JOURNEY TO INNER JOY AND SUCCESS IN REAL ESTATE

A book for realtors who want to enhance their perception of life and long to be inspired, rather than motivated.

YOANA NIN

"As you journey through life's ups and downs the story Yoana shares will inspire you to seek to find the best version of yourself in every situation life puts before you. Both heart reeling and mind strengthening thought are provoked when you dive into this incredible story of wanting more."

Coach Anna - International Business Coach
and founder at SuccessChanger.com

To the ones who make my life magical

I'm honored to dedicate this book to the ones I adore. To my husband Mihai, who always supported me regardless of what was going on in my head, our kiddos Anaïs and Phoenix- the most joyous, free souls I could have ever wished for, and my sweet parents and sister, the nucleus of my happy childhood.

Cu mii de multumiri...

Mama, tata, Andrada si Dorin,

Sunteti tot ceea ce am nevoie in aceasta viata! Sunteti sarea mea in bucate.
Va multumesc pentru tot! Va iubacesc!

Contents

Chapter One

From Dream to Soul Searching Agony

My current and forever name is Yoana Nin, but I came into this world as Ioana Anca Gliguta. I'm not sure if you actually need to know my real name, but I would never write a book and not mention it as I'm very proud of my Romanian origins. Gliguta is not a common name, and there are only a few people left in the North Western part of Romania, right at the border with Hungary. By nature, we are strong people; used to taking the bull by its horns, as my dad would say. We don't give up easily, we're passionate and we are loyal, family loving folks. As you noticed, Gliguta is not an easy name to pronounce, especially if your native language is English. Nin comes from Anaïs Nin, who is my all-time favorite author and a woman I wish I had known. Her freedom of speech and judgement are mind blowing to me. I read Incest after graduating University, while working as an Au Pair in New Jersey. I did not know at the time how that book would transform my life. I knew that if I was ever blessed with a baby girl, then her name would be Anaïs.

Even though we are very early into my story, what I will share is that when I received my citizenship, I was given the opportunity to change my name, so I chose a last name that meant something for me. Also, by then, I had already worked as an actress in Hollywood, as well as a script consultant, wardrobe person, and an assistant director, using Yoana Nin as an AKA; after my manager asked me to change my name to something easier to pronounce. The directors were not sure where to place me, and reading Ioana Gliguta was a hassle, so I was kind of "forced" into adapting for an easier professional path.

Nowadays, my alias is kick-ass mother, wife and realtor! I am also a cool girl overall, based on my own views on myself.

I have these big blue eyes, a big nose and dry, curly hair that is fifty percent gray. One might think it's too early to be this gray, but genes and intense thinking did it for me. As you can see, I am super humble, real, and I accept myself!

It's an honor to invite you into a short version of my life's journey. I hope that through my writing, you will break through your limitations and decide what your future in real estate will be (if any!). My story is neither complex nor unique. I'm pretty aware of this fact. But it's mine, and I share it with the pride and joy of a first-time writer. I don't look for perfection in this book, but I can assure you that every word is true.

The reason you are enjoying my writings is either because you know me already, or because you are a realtor who saw my superwoman marketing online. It's great that you are present and paying attention to what is going on in your industry. Especially in these hard times. Things are changing drastically with viruses and unpredictable shifts that can (if allowed), change our path. It's hard to make it in real estate, but hardship could also be a relative term. Everyone has different views on what hard means.

Just so you know, no matter what the situation is, I am ALWAYS GRATEFUL. I have many reasons to feel this way. I am awake; I feel my heart beating; I see the sun, the moon, the stars, I hear the traffic; I smell my Nespresso; I adore my family and I can drive to see clients. I could go on and on about the reasons, big or small, but I always feel gratitude in my heart.

Maybe one day I'll be able to sell my happiness at a fancy store. I would put my "Organic good mood" in a classy-looking bottle and enjoy watching the buyers transform their mindset.

Can you imagine? It would be a kick-ass achievement to make people want to carry that bottle with them everywhere. All they would need to do is drink a sip of good mood and see their life transform. Especially now, with this Coronavirus pandemic.

From a professional perspective, I can assure you that if a girl from Romania can write a book in English and make money in real estate (while still keeping sane), you can do it too. You will travel into my heart, and I hope that my honest vulnerability will help you understand that all it takes to be successful is meeting your own criteria for what success is. Just forget what everyone else says. Dance to your own music, listen to your OWN song!

You don't know how many times in my life I had the wrong song in my head. I had the impression that it was MINE, but I had borrowed it and made it sound like it was mine. Overall, copying someone else's rhythm and story sucks!

I had a dream about being the "One". Now, I could have dreamed I was Oprah because she is definitely THE ONE. Or, I could have dreamed that I was a princess, but I still somehow associate pink with NO, so being a princess was not my destiny either. Instead, my dream was vague but strong emotionally. It was confusing but made me wake up all sweaty and in awe. What does one do when you have this "surreal" presence in your body? I had no clue how to handle or interpret it.

The voice talking to me was the calmest I have ever heard. The light coming from that direction was strong, and all I heard was "You Are the One. You are the chosen one." I saw a woman who asked me if I recognized her. Based on my childhood, growing up as an Eastern Orthodox, I nodded and knew she was Mary.

"The most important point is to accept yourself and stand on your two feet."—Shunryu Suzuki

The Mary. She smiled at me and gave me a hug that still gives me the chills. Thank you, Mary, for always protecting me; for sending the angels to save me when I needed it–just like after I had the car accident at sixteen-years-old. My life is exactly how it should be. I don't need any proof. I feel it.

It took years of soul searching, sleepless nights and turmoil, and many more years of questioning what in the world I am supposed to do with my life. On the surface, I had it all! I have two amazing children, one killer husband and a great family (my parents, sister and her hubby rock), but there was a special need in me to go beyond, to look deeper into my soul. What was my power? Why did I come on this Earth? How can I serve? I had all of these questions. I had tried different ways to find the real voice when that organic feeling does not need to make an effort to manifest. I knew I had it in me, but it did not materialize into a definite concept for a very long time. It was not supposed to be something big, or something that yielded a lot of cash. All I can share with you is that through my life, I never looked at anything from a perspective of return on investment. I'm a super simple person. Please do not worry if you still don't know what you are supposed to do with your life. I mean it! It will come to you soon. Just listen closely.

I'll share my life's moments with you. I'll go deep, with no setbacks. There are no secrets to my journey to self-mastery, but rather pivotal steps that took some time and self-acceptance to implement and make my own. I hope that with your curiosity and hunger for discovery, I can open your mind to lead you towards your success.

"Our prime purpose in this life is to help others. And if you can't help them, at least don't hurt them"—Dalai Lama

I can assure you that when you finish reading this book (if you try), you will succeed in any aspect of your life you desire.

And do you know how I am so positive? Because you are everything you want to be already. But you just need a reminder...

When I was in elementary school, there was a big event at my school. My teacher asked all of us what we wanted to become when we grow up. I answered quickly, "I want to be an actress!" We still have that recording, which is awesome. During 1987, in Romania, few people could afford to own a camera. Luckily someone in the crowd had the privilege to own one, which was super cool. It's literally the only recording I have of myself during that part of my life. Every time I think back to those years of my life, I get very teary. Not because I feel that those were the best times, and I was so happy then. I get teary because I recognize the same girl in myself, and it feels amazing to know I did not lose my inner child. The cool thing is that I did actually decide to go for an acting career. My mother and father were not thrilled with my choice of making a minimal amount of money, especially during that time in Romania. Actors still do not make a lot in today's world, and the work and effort that the profession involves is not a joke. You either love it or hate it!

It is generally very difficult to get accepted into an acting university, which allows only ten new students per year. You read it correctly. Only ten! The exams one has to pass are very specific, and they involve acting related challenges that include music, dance, monologues, improv, etc.

"No one saves us but ourselves. No one can and no one may. We ourselves must walk the path."— Buddha

"But why would you decide on acting?" my father would ask. "Most actresses sleep with directors! You'll be on alcohol and everyone will think you are a slut." This type of reaction comes from fear of not being able to control something. Oftentimes, parents want to save us from something that they consider dangerous, but they forget that we do not belong to them. We have our own journey. Even though I knew they meant well, and they trusted me, it still didn't feel very good. I knew I had to fight with all I had to make them change their minds. It's a good thing that they did not react the same way when I got married. I guess by then they realized I was doing things my way. As I was determined to succeed, I dealt with their adversity and rejection well. I showed them my passion and commitment for the craft, and in the end, after one full year of going back and forth, they just gave up.

It is known that in an acting career, things can heat up quickly. I mean… they teach you how to undress and be naked in front of anyone and everyone. And you need to have an easygoing personality to be able to be naked in and out. I never cared about being naked. To be honest with you, I loved it. I loved the adrenaline of rushing backstage and changing quickly; that frenzy of touching up my makeup, the laughter and smell of cigarettes and smoke. All of those judgment free moments are rooted in my heart. They prepared me for what life would throw at me later.

I experienced some of the best years of my life between 1998 and 2002. The University of Theatrical Arts in Tirgu-Mures is still one of the best in the nation. And guess what? I never slept with anyone to get an acting gig. Never.

"We do not exist for the sake of something else. We exist for the sake of ourselves."—Shunryu Suzuki

Instead, I was sleeping with the script in my hand, in love with the smell of paper and printed dialogues. Every day I was falling more and more in love with the stage. My colleagues were awesome. I learned a lot regarding the work ethic that is required when so many people are involved. To create a play from A to Z, one needs a great deal of focus, vision and emotional power. Everything was happening with ease in my creative bubble. There were daily rehearsals, daily walks to university and back to the dorm, potatoes roasted in a rush, cold nights with hot wine, amazing masterminds and excellent teachers. I remember walking home from rehearsals with a friend, dancing to Frank Sinatra's Strangers in the Night. We felt fearless.

Can you hear my heartbeat? The passion is still there; it never left. It elevated my destiny and molded my body and mind into the woman I am today. Love is everything. The love I had for myself allowed me to live those years fully and to share happy thoughts with everyone around me.

If you are in real estate, no matter how tired or refreshed you wake up in the morning, or how you feel that particular day, your job is to deal with clients. Those clients have feelings! I know I didn't just hit you with something you had no clue about. But I honestly feel that when the word "lead" is used in this business, most people tend to forget that these potential money-making clients are just like me and you. We don't call them in the morning and say, "Hello lead! How's it going?"

I shared my acting experience with you earlier because I believe that it taught me discipline.

"I like to listen. I have learned a great deal from listening carefully. Most people never listen."—Ernest Hemingway

This helps me on days when I don't feel like getting out of bed or lead generating. But what exactly is lead generating in real estate? According to the dictionary, it is defined as, "a marketing term that describes the process of attracting and converting a prospect into someone who's interested in your products or services."

Ideally, you should shift from having to lead gen, to wanting to do it. You should want to bring your value to the table through unforgettable customer experience. Whilst I was in university, I learned how to listen to others. Not talking about you all the time is a huge part of anyone's life and future success. Ask questions about everything and pay close attention to the responses you receive.

In business, everything starts with passion, and then comes your drive! The capacity to understand others, listen to their needs and serve them with honesty is more important than any rationale. Your clients must enjoy working with you and you must always have their well-being in mind. If you direct your attention to providing value, then it will become easier to work on a deal. This will help you focus on that task for longer. Lighten up while you focus!

Here is a realtor question for you to answer. Have you ever woken up feeling excited about showing homes or going into a listing appointment? If you are a brand-new agent and have not been to an appointment yet, I highly encourage you to make yourself laugh before you go.

Jump up with the excitement of meeting a new client. It all starts with you and how you feel, even before interacting with that person.

"I believe you are your work. Don't trade the stuff of your life, time, for nothing more than dollars. That's a rotten bargain."—Rita Mae Brown

Put a smile on your face. Do you love working in real estate? Do you get that thirst to know all there is about it? A lot of people get into a particular job because they think they will make a lot of money. It must look very nice from the outside, driving expensive cars and all that jazz. While there is nothing wrong with any of that, you cannot fool your gut.

No matter how hard you try, there is no playing around with the universe and what it has in store for you. No matter how hard Tinker Bell tried, she still had to go back to being herself.

Chapter Two

Overcoming Life Challenges

I never applied to become a U.S. Green Card holder, but I won the Green card lottery! How was that possible? Now that I look back, I still can't believe the course of events and how much we had to overcome to make all this happen!

Meet Mihai Mocanu, my incredible husband. I've known him since I was 6 or so. We used to be neighbors in Satu-Mare. He used to be very preppy, while I was just another girl riding a bike. He never really looked at me, which was for a good reason. I'm 7 years younger, so while I was learning to add and subtract, he was dating pretty hot women and driving them in his German cars around town. I'm jokingly telling him now that I cursed him to say hello to me every day. He never really replied to all my desperate attempts to make him acknowledge my presence when I passed his home on my bike.

Talking about setting intentions. After I graduated university, in 2002, I decided to come to the U.S. for one year as an Au Pair. I wanted to have some fun and make a little bit of money. Before I left for New Jersey, I decided to throw a party to say goodbye to my friends and family. My dad was in charge of buying the beer, and he went to my husband's beer factory to check their selection. Mihai's family was pretty well off by Romanian standards. They had several restaurants as well. Since our families knew each other, it was normal for my dad to try their venue first. That day, after he got home, his ego seemed to be a bit hurt. He told me that our previous neighbors, the Mocanu family, did not remember me very well. How can their boy not remember his daughter Ioana? So all of a sudden, my father had the urge to remind the Mocanu clan who I was and what I looked like.

"Unexpected events can set you back or set you up. It's all a matter of perspective"—Mary Anne Radmacher

Despite my lack of time, I had to jump into the car and promote myself to my ex-neighbor and taste some beer, which should have already been bought by my dad! And there was my future hubby. Making alcohol. Living the life! We definitely had something going on when we looked at each other. Now I won't say I fell in love, but I did get a bit soft in my knees. I had a nice, brief conversation with him, got the beer and invited him to the party. He never came. A few days later he called and invited me for a swim at their lake house. The lake house was charming, and that first night together was something one cannot forget. We talked about everything, from life to present and future. There was a lot of laughter and wine. He also gave me a Lotus flower, picked straight from the lake. And that is the wonderful start to our love story. During the year to come, we were online day and night. He actually proposed via email and I replied "YES" without hesitation.

As an Au Pair, my experience was unbelievable! Mihai wanted to come and visit me, but they denied him a Visa. He was a young man, in university, so they must have thought he would come to the States and never return. Because of this, we did not see each other in person often. I went back home at Easter-for two weeks, and the engagement ring was given to me in a glass of wine. Original, huh? It's good that I didn't choke on it! We became real good friends.

After my final return home in 2003, everyone knew about my forever plans. Since it was pretty unexpected, a lot of my friends were doubting this would last.

I immediately started working as an actress. I missed the stage. But things don't always go as planned, right?

"We take life for granted, sleepwalking until a shattering event knocks us awake. Zen says, don't wait until the car accident, the cancer diagnosis, or the death of a loved one to get your priorities straight. Do it now."—

Philip Toshio Sudo

I'm sure I must have projected my intention to go back to the U.S. at some point in time. Even though we had everything we needed and our lives together were just starting, there was always a conversation that would somehow revolve around eventually moving to other countries.

We were soon in agreement about the 3rd of july, 2004, as our wedding date. We were eager and excited as there were a lot of great things happening all around us. We also decided to build a tiny house, just for the two of us. We had a little help from our folks and used some of the money each of us had saved. Just a few contractors, our parents and the two of us made the entire project come to life! I forgot to mention that Mihai is a material engineer, and he is super handy. He was adding brick and mortar every day. We both designed the entire house from scratch. Up to this day, it is a remarkable piece of architecture.

Before we moved in, we were swapping between our parent's houses. One night we were sleeping at my parents' house, the next at my future in-laws' house. Then the tragedy hit!

Around 11 p.m., while watching a movie, my husband complained about a headache. I did not take it seriously until the moment he put his pillow over his head and lost the power of speaking coherently. Twelve hours later, I was in an ambulance, crossing the border from Romania to Hungary-Miskolc to be precise. The reason for leaving Satu-Mare was plain and simple. The Romanian medical support and equipment did not support the type of testing that Mihai needed at that time.

My dad, with some of his high positioned friends in the medical field, arranged for this to happen. It was extremely rare for a Romanian citizen to be transported across the border to receive help. As a previous student, who graduated from the same city that was now helping him, Mihai thankfully still had his medical insurance. He needed immediate help.

Shortly after we arrived there, we were told his results were not good. He had meningoencephalitis.

According to Huntzinger (2007), Meningoencephalitis is a rare, late-stage manifestation of tick-borne ricksettial diseases, such as RMSF and Human monocytotropic ehrlichiosis (HME), caused by Ehrlichia chaffeensis (a species of rickettsiales bacteria). It took two full months of uncertainty. There were days when he was awake, and days when he was in intensive care. We never knew what room we would find him in upon our regular visits. We were traveling from Romania to Hungary three times per week. At one point, there was only Mihai and another young man in one secluded room from the intensive care section. As me and the gentleman's wife were looking at each other in despair, I remember thinking everything will be alright. Knowing nothing about the Law of Attraction, I undoubtedly knew that Mihai would get better. My husband was very positive, and despite his condition, he was making everyone around him laugh (he was printing food recipes for the nurses). Unfortunately for the other couple, the young man passed away within two days. It was the closest I had ever come to seeing someone die. I was heartbroken. But for us, the universe had different plans!

As Esther Hicks would say, "The best things in life happen when you don't beg for them, when there's no struggle involved." Always choose the path of least resistance.

After two months of intense stress of being tired from traveling and lack of sleep, I finally got a happy text message whilst I was in rehearsals, "My levels are way down. I think they want to release me this week. I miss you." Life is so fragile, and we really need to live it to its fullest potential. This is why it is essential to work on our perception and intelligence which can lead to us living a beautiful life. One thing that I have learned through years of difficult experiences is that liveliness is a key factor in determining healthy relationships and one's success.

Chapter Three

Leaving Safety Behind

Mihai's uncle was, and still is a great doctor. However, like many intelligent people, he wanted to leave Romania. Things did not go well financially for doctors who were honest and not willing to take bribes. There is too much to explain about the system-but in short, I'll share that even today, if you go to the doctor in Romania, it does not hurt to have some cash in your pocket. It's a reminiscence from communism and its hardship. Educated people struggle to have a decent life, while most politicians are corrupt and do little to help keep talent in the country. Romania seems to be falling apart, and it sucks!

The idea to escape and settle for better grounds was something that Mihai's uncle had been playing with for a long time. One day, he asked my husband to walk him through the process of applying for the Green Card lottery. Since he was not too tech "savvy," he had no clue how to change his picture online, make it the right size and all the other things that came with the application process. The Diversity Immigrant Visa program is one of the fastest ways to receive a U.S. permanent resident card. Many people still come to America through the lottery. As my husband was showing him every step, he decided to apply for ourselves as well. Why not? It was just for fun! That's what his gut feeling told him to do. We were not thinking about moving to the U.S., but we had talked about the possibility of maybe moving to Canada one day. Not soon, though! Our house was beautiful, filled with our vision and tasty decor. We had just moved in, and it felt great to start our lives together in the space we built with our own sweat. We loved that space!

As weeks went by, it was finally time to go on our honeymoon. Nobody was thinking about the lottery anymore.

The day Mihai helped his uncle apply was the last day anyone talked about it. This should help you to understand how insignificant winning the lottery was for our plans at that moment.

We had the Mediterranean Sea and the Sahara Desert for two weeks. We enjoyed riding the camels, eating unique food and savoring a culture that we had never experienced before. And of course, as every newlywed couple, we were building dreams together.

Upon our return to Romania, my father-in-law picked us up from the airport, and told us that he left a huge envelope on our kitchen table. He had no clue what it was, and almost threw it away, thinking it was some spam mail.

It turned out Mihai's uncle never won the lottery, but I did! All of those papers were there to bring us the most unexpected message from the Universe. We were in shock! We had been given a once in a lifetime opportunity to go to the land of opportunity. But on the other hand, we had to decide to leave our family and friends behind. As much as it sounded exciting, our souls were fighting now with a unique and emotional situation.

"Why do you have to go? Why do you need to go there? You have everything you need here. You will clean toilets. You will never make it! You will be back in a couple of months. You will starve. You will never succeed in anything, and your career will be finished before you know it. What will happen to your house? Do you realize there is nobody there to help you with anything?"

Understanding how difficult it was for our families to let go, we decided to be bold and leave. It was heartbreaking, but after a couple of months we said our goodbyes. We felt the spirit of adventure but had no clue what life would throw at us.

Congratulations to us for taking the step into the unknown This is the beginning of a journey that would teach us more than any book out there. We decided to look for what we wanted, and not in the direction of the lack of it.

After finding out that we won the green card lottery, a friend of Mihai's dad offered him a job as a logistics manager for his trucking company.

And it wasn't just about the money. We felt secure with the idea of working with "our" folks, with someone that "cared". We were provided temporary housing as well; a whole ranch-style home to ourselves. Initially, the people that offered the job did not make us pay rent. We had no clue of the real reason behind it! We later learned that they were paying my husband half of what their previous employee was making. They were Romanian businesspeople who came to the U.S. around fifty years ago and were making a good living. They were hard-working people who realized that my husband had the skill that they needed to grow their revenue. They will always be the first ones who gave us a helping hand, and we will always be grateful. We worked a lot to help them, and without them, we would have never continued our U.S. experience the way we did! Honestly, all we had when we arrived in the U.S. was ten thousand dollars. We worked hard in Romania to save up money and we never questioned whether it was going to be enough to survive.

For those of you who are curious, we were living in Redlands, which is a small city near San Bernardino, California. It was a nice place, filled with very rich families.

"From this point forward, you don't even know how to quit in life."—Aaron Lauritsen, '100 Days Drive.'

As we were settling, the hungry actress in me started looking for a theater company where I could perform. I knew I was not going to sit at home and read, cook or clean. My husband was given one week to get used to the U.S. time difference. We didn't have a lot of clothes in our suitcase to suit the weather in California. As we were getting used to everything, we started buying much needed summer clothes, food and cleaning supplies for our new residence which was kind of filthy.

For a long while, we were comparing the prices in Romania to those in the U.S., but we quickly learned that it was not healthy for our own sanity. As we were speaking in Romanian and Hungarian (my husband's mom is Hungarian and that's the language they speak at home), there were words that we learned not to say whilst out in public. We learned to not say "puszi" and "fac" in public as they sounded like inappropriate English words. "Puszi" means Kiss in Hungarian and "fac" means "to do" in Romanian. We were getting the "looks" from the public until we realized what was happening. At this point in time, we still have to be very careful about the words we use in public. We are trilingual in our household and the children do not realize how some of our words sound to locals.

I'll never forget the temperature shock of the air conditioning that took almost a year to overcome. Did you know that almost nobody in Romania has air conditioning? I'm sharing this with you, as immigrants have to adjust to so much. Most of the time, people don't understand how big the differences really are. When the Romanian employer picked us up from the airport, we immediately felt the cold air conditioning in the car, and I could not stop shivering in the back seat.

"A wise person should have money in their head, but not in their heart."—Jonathan Swift

That shiver stayed with me for months to come and whether it was Ralphs or Whole Foods, I was literally running into the store to buy groceries and running out of there as fast as my feet allowed me. It was hot outside and freezing inside!

We were talking to our family almost all of the time. Thank God for Skype! I missed my bed, my family, our food, and our game nights.

Romanian culture is a family loving culture, and none of our parents wanted to be that far from us. Now that I am a mother, I feel their pain and understand better. But I also understand that my children have their own path, and my goal is to let them fly wherever their heart desires.

I now have a much better understanding of how my parents felt when we left. Sometimes I miss my children while they are at school, and I find myself running to my car so that I can see their faces. It doesn't matter how tired I am, or how stressed I may feel, I simply want to hug them. I have to admit that it will be hard for me to completely let go when they move out.

"Consider the trees which allow the birds to perch and fly away without either inviting them to stay or desiring them never to depart. If your heart can be like this you will be near to the way"—Zen

Chapter Four

Achieving Takes Courage

The business that my husband was now learning was highly based on lead conversion. It was a transportation business; he was supposed to manage loading those huge trucks that you see on the highway. I'm sure you recall passing them; they carry cars, motorcycles and boats. When I say load, I mean that he was the one finding the units online and making sure the trucks were full at all times. He was also determining the routes from the East Coast to West Coast for each driver. With multiple routes per month, they were busy. Most shipments were ordered online (similar to Zillow lead capture), or referred to us by brokers who we had a business relationship with. The name, number and email of the person who wanted a unit shipped entered the database. Mihai would see what type of unit it was and load the trucks twenty-four hours a day, seven days a week. It took convincing every person to use the company he was working for. Even though they had a great reputation, the competition was very strong. It was extremely time consuming as every trip had to save the most amount of time and gas. Drivers would often complain about some routes that were not easily accessible (like mountains and other areas that were hard to get to). When my husband was employed, the company had two trucks and two drivers. After my husband became the logistics manager, the company started increasing profits day by day. It was busy! We were getting calls at the house at 5 a.m. from drivers on the East Coast who were experiencing issues with loading the units on the trucks. My husband was always on call, but with his calm way of handling things–everything was always handled professionally.

I found out that Redlands Theatre Festival was in the midst of rehearsals and there was a need for volunteers with costumes.

I immediately signed up and started going there daily. It was a humbling experience for me. I was not used to working backstage and had no experience in design. I had to work long days, clean up after a twelve-hour day and help with whatever had to be done. As an actress, these were things that I took for granted back home. Romania is not a country where volunteering is common. People barely survive with their work, so we are not very familiar with doing jobs for free. Regardless, I was super excited to be in my field of work, and my spirits were high! I was watching the rehearsals every time I had a minute. Being part of something creative, something that was uplifting, was filling me with joy. After seeing me there every day, the director started to warm up to me and asked me questions here and there. I shared with him that I had just graduated with a BFA in theater, a four-year program at a top university in Romania. He seemed pleasantly surprised. For the next few weeks, not much happened, besides small talk and intense costume work on my end. But then, from nowhere, he asked if we could have a short, private talk. He looked at me and said, "The Rosalind part is open. Would you consider auditioning for it?" I swear I thought I was dreaming. How was this possible? Me? No way! I later learned that they were unhappy with the girl that had the part and in the middle of rehearsals, they fired her. It was a risky move on their end, being so close to the opening night, but for me, this was surreal. I had a once in a lifetime chance. He told me to practice a monologue and see him the next morning before rehearsal started at 9 a.m. I jumped in the car, printed out the monologue, told my husband to leave me alone for the rest of the day and started saying the words repeatedly.

I was very familiar with the play. I had studied a lot of Shakespeare, so it was nothing that was new or strange from a character perspective.

However, I was unable to memorize it until next day. I remember thinking that my accent might be too strong. But I didn't care about it as I was not going to let the accent or anything else stand between me and that part. The next morning came, I auditioned and gave it my all. They informed me on the spot that I got the job. No more backstage work for me. No more costumes. Now, I had others do my makeup and prep my costumes. I was on a stage that smelled of wood, with lights on my face, music in my ears, lines I had to say and a character to create. I was myself one hundred percent. The play was a real success. My face was on the first page of the L.A Times within weeks of the premiere. Everyone was in awe. What happened to the "impossible"? Now you have an idea of how it all started.

After all the performances were over, I told my husband we needed to move to Hollywood. There was nothing happening in Redlands from an acting perspective, and I was pretty bored. We informed the Romanian family that we were moving, which created a bit of friction. By now, we were paying them rent, so the fact that they could not "control" us anymore was not ideal for their situation. But I did not discuss this subject too much. My mind was set. We were out! I have to say that in order for us to rent something; we needed their help to cosign the lease. We had no credit. Since Mihai was working for them, they didn't have much to say. It was too risky for them to argue with us and lose him as an employee.

Within two weeks, we rented a studio apartment, two minutes away from the Chinese Theatre (where the Oscars are held). I was starting to feel alive. Sweet was the year of 2006! I immediately found a Russian manager who sent me to a few auditions here and there. They were not impressive. However, I was represented. I signed up for all the casting websites, so I was regularly getting small gigs. I was Madonna's stand in, did hand double jobs, booked a featured part in Accepted, had a sexy dancer job in Kumi Koda's "Run for Your Life", and did some background work with Clooney, De Niro and Pacino. The list goes on and on. I was performing in great theater productions and got to become friends with Yennie Lam and Gabi Moreno who are amazing musicians. Gabi won the Latin Grammy award for best new artist, and Yennie Lam is well-known in the electric guitar world. I also had the honor of meeting Lizzie Maxwell, a fabulous actress and writer, and I learned the craft of script supervising.

The directors of her movie, Fixing Rhonda, were James Biberi and Nellie Scuitto. They also starred alongside Tessa Munro, who was the lead actress. We enjoyed hanging out with John Aniston (Jennifer Aniston's dad). He starred in Lizzie's movie as the detective. He was easy to work with and had a great sense of humor. What amazing memories

The goal was to get into Screen Actors Guild (SAG) to make more money and get better gigs. In order to get into SAG, you either had to get three SAG vouchers (and I only got two) or get a SAG part in a movie which was very hard to do once you were booked as a non-union actor. But even though I did not get my SAG status, I was featured in a national Chick-fil-A commercial. I made seven hundred dollars per day.

I could have NEVER imagined that much money from one day's worth of work! I learned that my goals were not negotiable, and anything can happen if one truly desires it.

Months passed, and we became busier every day. We even moved into a one-bedroom apartment, very close to our first studio. We were now paying a bit more per month, but we had more space. In Los Angeles, to have one thousand square feet is a huge deal.

As we moved into a new apartment, I felt the urge to have a baby. It was as spontaneous as a summer rain. In May 2007, I found out I was pregnant. By then, I had a lot of jobs. I had succeeded to get accepted into a great theater company, but none of it mattered.

My inner voice was taking me to motherhood, and I listened. My husband was still working for the same company, with the same people and pretty much no change in salary. The only difference was that now he had more things to do and more calls to make. So needless to say, we had to move to a two-bedroom apartment, as he needed a separate office for work. We moved to Sherman Oaks. My pregnancy was normal, but loaded with morning sickness, which stopped me from getting acting work done after the fifth month or so. I surrendered to doing housework and preparing for the big event.

Before the New Year, my parents came to stay with us for a few months, and help us with last minute preparations. We were so excited that they were able to come for such a long period of time!

We had game nights, went on long walks, went to the beach and made a bunch of Romanian food. On January 23rd, at 11 p.m., my water broke. Over the next 17 hours, until the magical 4:16 p.m., I experienced the most excruciating pain I have ever felt in my life. It turned out that my platelets were very low, to the point where I could not get the epidural. I did not dilate at all until 11 a.m. (despite the fact that I walked most of the night), which is when the doctor decided I needed to be induced. It felt like someone was stabbing me with ten knives at once.

Then her heartbeat dropped. Suddenly they put an oxygen mask on my face, and I was surrounded by five doctors. "Ioana, push that baby out now!" I gave birth to Anaïs, a perfectly healthy and beautiful girl. Her skin was perfectly clear; her hair was black and silky; her face was pure perfection, and she immediately held my finger and latched to my breast. How can a mom completely forget the trauma when she sees her newborn? It's such an amazing feeling and an honor to be a mother.

Now let me share something very funny with you. This should be remembered as "one of the funniest birth stories of all times." My dad had decided to not go to the hospital when my water broke. He stayed home, and only my mom joined us. After Anaïs was finally out, we suddenly saw him in the hospital room, looking very red and sweaty, and kind of agitated. While holding Anaïs and being in awe about how beautiful she was, I could not resist asking my dad why he was there. How did he get there? He never drove a car in the U.S. Also, how did he know where the hospital was? We found out that my mom, who was tired and upset about how hard this was for me, told the poor man that he should have been there. As soon as I saw him in the room, I felt that something was not right.

The poor guy jumped into the car, somehow followed my mom's instructions, got to the hospital (it was only a couple of miles away), and parked in the covered parking structure. However, when he wanted to exit our two door Mazda sports car, he could not open the doors. They were locked. He was so panicked that he got out of the car through the small front window, which he somehow managed to open. Can you imagine? He is two hundred pounds. His belly alone is bigger than the window! To this day, we remember that when we saw him in the hospital room; we knew something was not normal. He only shared his "adventure" with us a bit later on, so we could actually crack up "in peace".

This is real parental involvement! I am sure that my dad found it difficult to get out of the car headfirst. He scratched his belly and his hands, but he did not care at all. The sacrifices one makes for his children.

We were very overwhelmed by being new parents! The journey was intense, with no sleep for months (maybe 2 hours per week or so). My milk didn't come in until a good week after delivery, and the baby was screaming, hungry. I was advised to only keep her at the breast and not give her formula. I could not sit up due to hemorrhoids, and I almost got mastitis. Mihai was on the phone with drivers all day as he had no time off, and my parents did their best to help as much as they could. But the time came when they had to return to their own lives in Romania. They needed to get back to their own jobs, and to my sister, who was in college at the time. And that's when I realized that it would take some time until I could work as an actress again.

"If you don't understand what unconditional love is, when you become a parent it all makes sense."—Kate Summers

I dedicated a lot of time to Anaïs, while helping my husband as much as I could with his work. He was getting to be very challenged by working for the same people as now they had increased the number of trucks he was loading and barely increased his pay. They were very demanding and did not respect his time off. He never got to take any vacations and that had to stop.

All Coasts Transport was born on a day like any other day. I woke up, got dressed, and went to the city to open a company. This is how you do it! You need to take ACTION. I didn't know what name to give it or anything about legal implications. I chose All Coasts Transport because it begins with A, so I thought it would be good for Google Search Engine Optimization (I know, right?).

That was the beginning of our own brokerage in transportation. Period. Done. I went home, told my husband he should quit and carried on with my day. Too much thinking and analysis is the enemy of following your gut.

Our destiny was in our own hands. They did ask him to stay (and told us we will never get anywhere!). But by now, we had the knowledge to be on our own-and all the drivers and brokers loved working with us.

Our own company was born, and I was in charge of calling leads and notifying them of the change. Also, as new orders were coming in, I was handling all the financial details of their shipment. I was working in my own time and taking care of our baby girl. We were definitely in sync with the news and what was happening in the U.S. during those times, but things were rolling for us and we did not give it too much thought. The subprime mortgage crisis was definitely taking over the U.S. We were aware of the crisis but we did what we did what we had to do to keep our family afloat.

"The critical ingredient is getting off your butt and doing something. It's as simple as that. A lot of people have ideas, but there are few who decide to do something about them now. Not tomorrow. Not next week. But today. The true entrepreneur is a doer, not a dreamer."—Nolan Bushnell, Entrepreneur.

Chapter Five

The Shift

My biggest and strongest desire as a new mother was to be able to provide the same quality of life that my parents gave me and my sister. I have noticed that as adults, people start acting more like their parents, even though not consciously. Have you ever noticed that about yourself? I imagined the same lifestyle with homemade fresh food on the table, the amazing smell of baked pies, the peaceful afternoons, and play times without organized playdates (we did not have those in Romania).

As months passed by and the workload was growing, it was getting harder to do it all! I was a mom, the cleaning lady in the house, the cook for the family, and a businesswoman. Man! Not complaining, but life was peachy! My sleep deprivation was definitely affecting our relationship. I had forgotten what real intimacy felt like. It was further than Antarctica for me. We were waking up every morning, feeding our baby girl, taking her to the park, working all day to tighten our relationship with our clients, but it was hard to have it easy. Money was coming in, though. And while we were struggling with maintaining the work/life balance, we also made the decision to buy a house.

Since all we had to do to qualify was exist, we decided to move to Valencia; to the city of Santa Clarita. We did extensive research before deciding on that area. We had to move quickly because our neighbors were very loud at night and the ambulances were waking Anaïs up all the time. We needed a home with an office that was not on the main road. It was not the best decision from a financial perspective. But who knew how bad things were going to get.

"We are being done. One might think we create and do it all, but I think it's backwards. Things happen as they should, in the moments they are supposed to happen."—Yoana Nin

Our to-do list was amplified every day, but we owed our little one a peaceful life; free from the noise of traffic or ambulances waking her up from her nap. We owed her a loving, calm, happy life, and that came with buying appliances, furniture, turning on utilities, getting new carpet, cleaning and upgrading stuff that was not to our liking.

Valencia was the first address that we belonged to, or that belonged to us, in the U.S. It was a two-bedroom with a loft, main pool views and across from the park and YMCA. It was also within walking distance to the mall. We were in Heaven! Our mortgage was around twenty-three hundred dollars, and taxes were astronomical. So, we had to make sure money was coming in. I'm sure most people understand the pressure. We were now growing our client database and our online profile as a new business.

We built our website and slowly started to create a name for ourselves as a family-owned small business. One day at a time! We made slow progress, but we had the right mindset!

You will notice that those who speak most of prosperity, have it. Those who speak most of health, have it. Those who speak most of sickness, have it. Those who speak most of poverty, have it.

You get what you think about, whether you want it or not. The way you feel is your point of attraction, and so, the Law of Attraction is most understood when you see yourself as a magnet getting more and more of the way you feel. When you feel lonely, you attract more loneliness. When you feel poor, you attract more poverty. When you feel sick, you attract more sickness. When you feel unhappy, you attract more unhappiness.

When you feel healthy and vital and alive and prosperous—you attract more of all of those things.—Esther & Jerry Hicks, The law of attraction: The Basics of the Teachings of Abraham.

Anaïs was growing and bringing laughter in our lives. She was and IS such an amazing girl! After a year or so, I felt like going back to acting. Being on the stage was calling me. I auditioned to become part of a reputable theater company, and I was accepted. It was a hard decision to be part of that company as it was located in downtown Los Angeles. The drive itself was strenuous for me. The long waits on the highway, while already being tired with work and the baby, were difficult to handle.

My schedule was getting too busy, and our daughter had a very clingy personality; every time I left the house there was a crying and screaming episode. She was not ready to let go easily. And then THIS happened. At the end of the year, I got pregnant again.

With love and joy, with eagerness and boldness, we welcomed another soul into my body. This pregnancy was very different though. I was sick most days and was barely getting out of bed. Needless to say, I had to quit acting. Daily family activities were not easy to accomplish with the state I was in. I kept my smiles up, but I was not feeling well at all. Not too long after my ten-week doctor checkup, I lost the baby in the bathroom. Alone. Devastation, sorrow, we felt them deeply. It's hard to deal with this type of loss. I was not prepared for it, and even though I've aged and listened to Esther and Abraham Hicks quite a few times so far, it's still taking me a few seconds to snap out of that painful memory. Are there any moms out there feeling the pain? As a couple, we did our best to continue life as it was.

There was no looking back and no painful conversations. Over time, my mood improved, and I was back to my old self. Once you go through a miscarriage, you learn about how often they happen, and you talk to other women that have experienced your pain. Like with any challenge in life, opening up really helps. And all the moms in the park were there supporting us. My family, along with all the people that helped us through the hard times, are the best!

In 2010, we started traveling more often. From a work perspective, being on the road was never an issue for us. I was answering calls while Mihai was driving. He would stop when he had to do something online, but overall our vacations were great.

We traveled to Romania to see our parents; we went to Croatia and visited the California coasts. Simply put, we were having the time of our lives, enjoying each other and what we had achieved up to that point in time. I recall going to Hollywood Bowl with a picnic basket, eating cheese and drinking wine.

I was finally done breastfeeding after two years and I welcomed adulthood, experiencing life (and a sip of alcohol), which was refreshing. Mihai and I had more fun together, and we started flirting again, like during those good old times. Every relationship goes through stages, but it's important to let the other person just be. 2010 was coming to an end, and we were back on our feet, strongly packed.

A lot of things happen around my birthday. When I was about 5, I was living with my parents in the condos of Satu-Mare. I was a tomboy and enjoyed playing outside in the sun. It was around my birthday, on a cold, January afternoon when I discovered something special. My favorite flower; The Snowdrop. It peeked out of the snow while I was building a snowman.

"Go to a place within yourself.
It's all perfect"—Yoana Nin

It was so gorgeous and delicate that I just stood there watching it for a long time. I covered it so people wouldn't hurt it. I believe that day was one of the first breakthrough moments in my life. I love that I can see perfection in everything.

So just like that snowdrop, I was ready to peek into the pregnancy world again, ready for new beginnings, with no stressful thoughts whatsoever. Little did I know that this decision would literally shift the course of my life.

On January 7th, I gave myself the present of wanting another baby. At thirty-one years old. It was a defining moment.

"I'm pregnant," I told my parents a month later. My mother was a bit reluctant at the news, but I knew that in her heart, she was happy for us. I remember my sister's face being warm and supportive, as only she could be. My dad was intimidated but Mihai's parents were thrilled. For my mother-in-law, this was the best news ever because she loves children. As the months rolled by, I enjoyed the beauty of every second of my pregnancy. My fully alive, fully present, fully pregnant belly was showing, and the baby was kicking. It was time to go on a two week vacation to Hawaii. I forgot to mention that we had purchased a time-share, amid all the years of discovering new lifestyles. We purchased it in 2007, before Anaïs was born. It is in Fort Lauderdale, Florida, and we use it every year as an exchange. That's how we are able to see new places at half the cost. I won't go into the time-share details, but overall, for us, it still works pretty well.

The price to go to Hawaii for two weeks, in May, was not very high. We had a wonderful trip! The food, weather, and discovering the island made us fall in love!

"Life is suffering."—Buddha

Anaïs learned how to swim underwater, all by herself. We visited the monastery and the monk there came outside and gave Anaïs an orchid. He looked at us and just smiled, peacefully. The people that witnessed our encounter with him told us it is very rare that he interacts with visitors. We were humbled by his presence. We returned home on a Saturday, feeling relaxed and ready to get back to reality. It was the first vacation without any outside pressure from the boss. Mihai felt recharged as well! As we got home from the airport, I unpacked and gave my daughter a bath.

Then I laid next to her in bed to help her go to sleep. My back started hurting as I was turning, and I thought it was because of the plane, and generally, the pregnancy. I was pretty far along at that point. As the time passed, my pain was getting worse. I could barely stand, so I asked my husband to give me a massage. It was 11 p.m.

After he went back to sleep, I had to use the restroom which brought the unthinkable. Again! Blood started pouring out of me like wine and I heard myself scream for help, urging him to bring some towels and call the ambulance.

Among all the distress, I had the power to call my friend Cassandra, who lived in the same neighborhood. She immediately came with her son to sleep at our house while Mihai joined me in the ambulance. Anaïs could not be left alone. My head was spinning, but I was trying to keep still and wait for the ambulance. I remember the feeling of being lost and empty-headed. I had strong feelings of incapacity to move, to react, or to think. They had to take him out of me. He was dead.

"You never know how strong you are until being strong is the only choice you have."—Cayla Mills

I had lost half of my blood. I never saw his face, never touched his hands, never saw his smile, never heard him cry, and I never ever hugged him. Our Jazz was not with us anymore. I felt lost.

I'll never forget my parents calling me all the time. Not being able to be with me was making them go insane. It was hard to tell people to just leave me alone, especially since at the hospital they kept on asking questions about our intentions, grieving strategy, and future counseling. I did not want any of that. All I needed was silence. A couple of days later I recovered, and we were released. There was my sweet girl wanting to play at the park, and there was me wanting to disappear, but disappearing was not the way to go.

We decided to leave California the day they sent his footprints in the mail, along with other baby items. I told Mihai I had to leave immediately, not knowing where we would go or how it would happen. I didn't care about our mortgage, offices, or any of the details because I instinctively knew I had to change gears, otherwise I would have fallen into depression.

I felt it very close. Within three weeks, we were out of Valencia, on a new adventure. It was our first trip ever without a destination, in our Honda Odyssey. We asked the universe for a renter and she showed up in our lives, rented our place for one year and purchased all our furniture. I could have pondered over whether it was safe to leave. I could have created setbacks. I had good reasons to just take it easy, but my desire to get out of that state was stronger than the will to play it safe. Safety is not one of my favorite words. A fresh start was awaiting. Thank you, Jazz, for helping me through this start. Mama loves you dearly and thinks of you often. I know you are here watching over these pages.

"When you understand that good and bad, everything and nothing are just a perception, you know the secret."—Yoana Nin.

Chapter Six

All You Have is TODAY

We had one year to travel; to live outside of our home in LA; to experience new places; new people, and new state parks. I swear that just thinking back to the day we got into our Honda Odyssey gives me goosebumps. But in that moment-there were no tender feelings; we were ready to leave. All I was concerned about was setting up the GPS to a first lunch stop, and getting the snacks, toys and books in place for Anaïs who was in the backseat. She had just stopped napping, but I was very clear in my intention to have her nap every day, in hopes that the drive wouldn't be too much. Again, we had no idea how long it would all take or what areas we would visit. We had absolutely no clue. We just put gas in the car and started driving north. Oh yes. The only thing we were aware of was that we wanted to go to the East Coast, as we were hoping for a more architecturally pleasing city. We knew we had the apartment leased for one year, but we did not necessarily plan on moving back after that year. I just wanted to go for as long as it took to heal. On another note, we missed the European vibe a lot!

Since watching movies and reading books as a child, Colorado, Chicago, the Grand Canyon and New York are places that have always attracted my attention. These were the places that I always wanted to visit. Even though our trip had no set timing, we were hoping for a couple of months on the road. Our living in the moment lifestyle was only going to end if we literally had to stop for some urgent reason. The days were passing; the car was moving, and the naps were not happening. The places we visited were beautiful. We successfully made it through two weeks of parks, camping, hiking and trying new foods and delicious ice cream in downtown Aspen. As much as we loved the Grand Canyon, we only stayed for one day and then we moved on.

With every day that was passing, we were struggling more and more with work and following up. We were getting stressed as there were many areas with no cell reception or internet, meaning the drivers couldn't reach us and vice versa. We were dealing with important shipments, like bikes that had to make it to Florida for a once in a lifetime event, or cars that were luxury and had to be well taken care of while transported in enclosed trailers. Deadlines were important in the shipping industry. While we were having the time of our lives, we suddenly got a call from the police. We were told that they were informed of a car being stolen while it was shipped with All Coasts transport. That was a bit intense! The rest of our days in the car were not as fun anymore, and Mihai's aggravation was affecting us all. Even though we had done nothing wrong, lack of proper communication made it hard for us to find out that one of the drivers-the one with the so-called stolen unit-had been stuck under a bridge for the past two days because of a tornado. The owner kept calling us and the driver, but we were in an area with bad reception and after one day of not hearing back, he called the police. That particular car was supposed to arrive in time for a luxury car event. It did not happen. But man, the stress of dealing with it was major. It was time for us to quickly determine where exactly we were going to stop.

While on the phone with a friend back in Valencia, I asked her for advice. Where should we go? She mentioned Chapel Hill, North Carolina, as she was from the area. As a realtor, I have never worked with anyone that moved to a different location for no specific reason, or because they were told to do so by a friend.

Whenever people ask me why we moved here, I try to be as short as I can.

So, I say that our move was not intentional, but rather something that just happened. After my friend's advice, we "Googled" for the best places to live in the U.S. The results showed that Raleigh, North Carolina, was a top-rated area from a perspective of schools, moderate climate and affordability. So this was the state that we chose.

The day we entered the state of North Carolina, it was pouring down with rain. We hadn't seen rain like that for years. My daughter was looking at a type of rain that she had never seen in LA. "Mom, what's this?" she asked when lightning and thunder made us reduce the speed as nobody was moving on the highway. We rented a two-bedroom apartment in Cary. We had a gym, a pool, and we were close to shops. After getting used to the area, we were surprised to see that homes were selling for two hundred thousand dollars.

We calculated that the mortgage on such a house would be equal to our rent. So, in our spare time we started looking at homes online and we concluded that if we found something great, we would break the lease a bit early.

Being self-employed can be challenging when you own a condo in California and you want to purchase a second residence in Cary, North Carolina. We were paying four hundred dollars on top of what our renter was paying in Valencia, by the way! Rent was twelve hundred dollars, and we had around forty thousand dollars in our savings account.

All Coast Transport was going well, but not excellent. We were used to making eight thousand dollars per month, which was a huge accomplishment for us! But as time passed, we were now in the five thousand dollars per month range.

Regardless, the constant thought of buying a house never left us, so we hired a realtor to help with our search. He was living in Chatham County at the time and I have no clue why he accepted working with us since he was very far from Cary.

Maybe he thought we would find something fast? My new hobby was adding favorite homes to the Multiple Listing Services and making long lists out of the properties that looked in fair shape. I was savvy and loved researching everything about every house.

At some point in 2012, our renter in LA told us she will need to move out fairly soon, as she could not afford to pay us the rent anymore. It didn't make much sense to us, but we trusted the fact that we would find somebody else. We had a few months left. The good news was that we were approved to purchase a new home!

Little did we know what the future had in store for our family. We had huge medical bills despite our health insurance. The loss of the baby brought expenses that kept on piling up and the money was short as the days were passing. We really didn't pay too much attention to the recession as we had our own drama to surpass. Even though we were reading the news, it did not affect us too much, or so we thought. But as we were set on buying a house and terminating the lease, I did notice that the amount of leads that were coming in was lessening. I had to increase my daily calls to potential clients. Our routine of booking units and loading the trucks was changing. Drivers were calling us asking for business and we were calling the companies who were selling the leads to ask for more business. Something was not quite right. Regardless, on April 9th, 2012, we closed on our house in Cary.

This day needs to be mentioned as at the closing table, our agent gave me a book. It was Gary Keller's, The Millionaire Real Estate Agent. He told me he saw the fire in me and that he thinks I should pursue real estate as a career. As we were going home from the closing, I looked at my husband and told him that I was signing up for real estate classes. With the new thrill in my heart and with my burning desire to become a realtor, it didn't take me long to find a school and register for classes. Our entire family from Romania came to help us move into our new home. We all get together in times when one needs support. That's how things are done. The lease was terminated.

We were doing daily trips from the apartment to the house with pots and pans, furniture, and all the other things that needed to be moved into the new location.

While Mihai was working on changing carpets and such, I was working on All Coasts Transport on my own while studying for real estate school.

We ended up changing windows, adding hardwood floors, painting everything, and upgrading bathrooms all on our own. My husband and his dad were the contractors. We hired someone to add skylights. Most of the money from our savings was now gone. Not smart at all! On top of everything, we could not find a renter for the LA condo. Prices in Valencia dropped dramatically. Business was not coming in so, needless to say, we were getting anxious. Everything was happening so fast and in between renovations, school and work, we realized the urgency of getting rid of the condo. We could not afford to pay two mortgages! We had to do a short sale. Our income and our monthly bills did not support our situation anymore. We had to start something that resembled a battle with the system.

We were now facing so much uncertainty. As much as I was trying to keep it together with schoolwork, taking care of Anaïs while Mihai worked on the house, dealing with California law and short sale procedures, it was very intense. In October 2012, the landlord put a lock on our place while the renter was still moving out. She still had belongings in there.

Here's the copy of our email that we sent to the company. Please note that some details have been removed for confidentiality reasons:

To whom it may concern;

Hello, my name is Ioana Gliguta, and along with Mihai Mocanu, my husband — are the owners of the property in Valencia, CA. With this letter I would like to inform you that by changing the locks at my apartment you have violated California state law! My tenant still had legal right to enter the property and was in the process of removing her things. The apartment was not vacant! Without any default notice, you have sent somebody to literally close my tenant out of her place and left her and two children without their belongings! We have begun the short sale process with our agent, Bob, and we have also received an offer on the apartment. The notices that we have been receiving from you clearly stated that we need to pay you by the date of 7/12/2012, date after which we will be in default. The short sale process began before that date. Now, because of your action, we are being held responsible by the tenant and not only that, your company will be held responsible both financially and legally for this action! We need you to immediately send someone to remove the lock as my tenant needs her things!

I, Ioana Gliguta have called you several times, talked to T.J and left our account manager multiple messages and I received no call back! It has been a week now from 7/10/2012- the date when you decided to lock our tenant out. Last time (Friday 7/13/2012) I talked to one of your representatives, I was informed that a manager will proceed with opening the locks faster.

Nothing happened yet! Again, your action, without a notice from your part to either me or the tenant- will have to be solved and your company will be held accountable for the pain that you are causing to both families. Please be advised that I need someone to contact us ASAP!

Thank You in advance,

Ioana Gliguta

Among the craziness, there was one positive. I eventually got my license as a provisional real estate broker.

The Mainsail home was looking lovely, but our bank accounts were almost empty. One morning, we were looking at our laptops as absolutely nothing was happening with our work. There were no drivers or leads, which meant no business. We were graciously welcomed to the most frightening recession in U.S. history. That month we made an amazing two thousand dollars.

"There is nothing more dreadful than the habit of doubt. Doubt separates people. It is a poison that disintegrates friendships and breaks up pleasant relations. It is a thorn that irritates and hurts; it is a sword that kills."— Buddha Siddhartha Guatama Shakyamuni

It was close to the end of 2012, and that day, that ugly cry, the desperation to find a source of income in order to survive, has left a mark in my heart forever.

And remember, I had everything that I needed back home. There was no reason for me to cry or be desperate because I could have gone back to Romania anytime and have it all-a house, money, support. However, that was not something that I even thought about.

I started applying for jobs and was rejected for everything. My schedule with my daughter did not allow me to work full time, so no job was willing to hire me on my terms. Plus, I had no qualifications other than a BFA in theater and film. Being a mom, a great person, friendly, and cute were not qualities that could help me get a job. So we called my parents. We asked them to help if they could, as at this point, there was barely anything coming in. The companies that were selling us the leads were not answering our calls. They were also broke. We had no clue what was going on.

My parents saved us. They managed to send us ten thousand dollars. That's what we had. That's how much we came to the U.S. with, in the beginning. It was our magical number. It gave us two months' worth of survival. I started looking at companies to join, and after visiting multiple offices, I signed with Keller Williams. It was December 2012. Before I started though, I told everyone in our group of friends that I'd be a realtor. I'm a social butterfly! I knew a lot of Romanian and Hungarian people who were park friends. It was the universe that helped me with setting up my next chapters. The universe, my family and my open mind.

"Create the highest grandest vision possible for your life, because you become what you believe."—Oprah Winfrey

Since I had no clue about anything real estate related, I had to understand that I was my own boss, and there was no babysitting involved. Just minimal help. The expenses that came with signing up with Multiple Listing Services and Raleigh Regional Association of Realtors were not low. Every cent counted against our monthly food and survival.

In the meantime, Mihai decided to sell All Coasts Transport. As soon as he started advertising, a lady called and offered him eight thousand dollars. As we were down to barely anything, he agreed to sell it to her. Three months later, we were notified that she'd been diagnosed with cancer, and didn't have long left to survive. So, do you think life is happening by chance? I was going back and forth to the office and already had potential clients lined up. Receiving the eight thousand dollars was like a dream come true. She had to come into our lives. Barbara had to be there, as a guardian angel. Signs are everywhere. All it takes is listening, sharpening the senses. Mental constipation can be torture, and the solution comes when you take the proper inner step. The source of joy or misery is within YOU!

Chapter Seven

Real Estate: A Blessing

I often hear real estate agents say that the "Grind is real." I have to admit that I'm not sure I agree with this whole grind thing. It might just be that I don't like the word, but it involves something that needs so much effort in a way that just does not come naturally. I agree with working towards your dreams and manifesting your desires, but I also agree that when you send a message out there focusing on what you don't have, that's what you will get more of! Nobody ever said accomplishing mastery is easy, but many people agree that there's no stress in this world, merely people thinking stressful thoughts. Esther Hicks, a wonderful inspirational speaker, advises that we should take the path of least resistance. Take the easy way, and don't stress too much! Relaxation will allow the Law of Attraction to help you do the things you actually want to do.

Most days, through all the craziness and uncertainty, I saw an opportunity. I am the type of person who reacts well to stress. Challenges inspired me to learn more, to adapt, and never give up. I will not deny that I often needed long walks to breathe deep and release the negative energy that all the new situations were bringing along. But I took every day as a new day, and instinctively I just bounced back, becoming stronger and stronger.

The office had hundreds of agents; they were really good realtors from all over the country. I was among top producers in the industry. I started taking all the Ignite classes, and everything else that was supposed to prepare me for the new career. I was running back and forth trying to get help to set up my profile, the Customer Relationship Management (that was a hot mess to be honest) and Dotloop to upload the documents for compliance.

I was creating business cards, signs and logos, determining the name I would use for my new business. None of these came easy! The issue was that I already had transactions lined up, but I did not know how to even open a lockbox. I had to find an agent to assist a bit with my showings and to teach me how to open a house. I paid her one thousand dollars for two brief visits to homes with my clients. I asked a couple of questions, paid the money and moved on. The one thousand dollars did teach me how to open the door to my future. Let's just interpret it this way! I would have expected to get at least the very basic help for free from my office, but the answers I was getting often sounded like "this agent is too busy" or something similar. Now that I look back, I wonder why it took me so long to leave that office. I made some amazing friends, but overall, I feel like I should have left when there was nothing else to learn. But each chapter molded who I am right now, so there is no looking back and no regrets.

Assissting clients with home purchases and sales became like an addiction after a few deals. It was obviously income driven initially, but I found myself always thinking about it, regardless of the financial outcome. How do I grow? How can I differentiate myself? Who do I love working with?

One day, I found myself door knocking. All our neighbors knew about me and my new career and I was proud to tell them about my husband and how he is so amazing at marketing and photos. My phone started ringing off the hook. One neighbor needed to buy and sell; a mom from the park needed advice on buying new construction; a lead from an open house was enquiring about the best schools, and a for sale by owner decided to list his home. It got to a point where I even met clients in stores.

The opportunities were everywhere. I was working ten to twelve-hour days.

Since I had never been too tech savvy, having Mihai on my side was definitely a huge help. I cannot tell you how much his knowledge helped and still does. Even though he was able to help me with setting up all the pages online, he was not licensed, and I was on the road all the time. Then, I was coming home and negotiating offers. During morning hours, I would spend two to three hours calling people to follow up with my contacts. It was the lead generating routine that I was taught. Since I am an actress and I know what a script is, you would expect me to be a huge script fan, but I never was. On the contrary, I was calling people I had never talked to and just openly, genuinely ask them to give me a chance, meet with me and decide if they would like to hire me. I understand that not everyone is comfortable with my technique, but the goal is to always do things that make you feel good.

The secret to having a successful phone conversation lies in ease, respect, and attitude. If you believe in yourself, you can make magic happen. I would start my conversations with, "Hello, I bet I'm the fiftieth agent calling you today. Can you handle one more minute? I promise no BS!" It would put people into a good mood and after three seconds they would all start complaining about being called by all these agents. But the worst part was that they would say hateful things about realtors, and I had to understand that the job I just landed was not a top respected one, but rather one that was associated with a bad reputation. Most people do not understand how difficult this job is! Regardless, I took action. Every second, every week, every month, a new client.

I had grits. It's the same as now. I was hungry for knowledge and still am! After about six months or so, we started thinking about how busy we were getting, and my husband was slowly considering getting his license as well. There was no magic pill for lead gen and conversion besides the typical "get yourself out there" attitude and hours on the phone. If I had given up every time someone yelled, hung up, or told me to fuck off, I would have been a coward. I politely apologized and did not call again. I don't believe in being disrespectful! My non-sales mind and heart can only do so much when it comes to pushing people. I need to benefit beings and not be motivated by self-cherishing thoughts and attachment. The more you let go of the idea of making money, the better you will feel overall. Craving admiration and approval is normal, but success comes when you focus on providing value from the heart. Yes, you can attract more transactions but don't get too attached to this. Just do it with ease. Don't have any fear and be grateful. If you are not happy with the little you have now, why do you think that more transactions will bring you happiness?

Everyone in the office was in overload mode. The one girl who had some knowledge of technology was also checking loops and documents for compliance.

The OP was always super tied up, and the agents were running around. I found joy in meeting new people and I was looking forward to the Tuesday team meetings. The atmosphere in the office was nice, and everyone was looking forward to it. I don't think I fully understood that I was really on my own. I was always looking for support. I totally understand how new agents feel. I had this goal of one hundred thousand dollars as an income. I knew we needed the money, and I had to compensate for these non-producing months.

So, one hundred thousand dollars was the minimum requirement for the year. Since I was so busy, I didn't have the time to learn all the ins and outs of the software. I kept asking the girl who was handling finances how much money I had coming in. I have to add that parts of the Gross Commission Income reports that were on the website were not accurate and up to date most of the time. Instead of wasting my time with refreshing pages, looking at all the things that were not functioning properly, I was asking Leah. Easy! She must have thought I was nuts, but as usual, I was just being myself. I was paying loads of money after each check on top of the monthly fees. The company was not providing any clients. Not even one. I've heard of other companies that were providing leads, but my company only had the calls that were coming into the office. The front desk would make a park retrieve announcement and whoever was in the office and was faster to respond–got the lead. We were like fish fighting for bait. Man, I do not miss that part at all.

As a mother and a wife, I felt exhausted. I had no real system and I spent most of my time multitasking. Whilst cooking, I was texting clients; whilst bathing, I was answering emails, and whilst playing on the trampoline, I was taking two minute breaks for quick phone calls.

It felt that I was doing too many things at once, which was one hundred percent true; every single task was on us, on me and my husband. In all honesty, I learned a lot in a very short period of time, but the most important thing I learned is that a lot of agents prepare a lot and almost never get things done. They spend too much time analyzing with too little action, and real estate is a business for doers.

"The secret of health for both mind and body is not to mourn for the past, nor to worry about the future, but to live the present moment wisely and earnestly."—Bukkyo Dendo Kyokai

Who you are does not depend on the money you make. Have you ever asked yourself what people will say at your funeral? Have you had scary thoughts about not being enough? How do you feel about yourself? Do you love your wrinkles, your hair, and your style? Would you hire yourself? Are you happy? Do you live in the moment or do you always think about yesterday or tomorrow? I was already who I wanted to be before I started real estate. I did not have to make money to BECOME someone...

I did not have the right experience, and if you are a starter agent, it's important to take action rather than always prepare to have the right experience. If you are really determined to get into real estate and serve others, you will figure it out. Just get it done. Get out of your comfort zone!

I was definitely being noticed in the office. I was full of energy, vibrating love, trust and compassion. Everyone who was interested in a small conversation would get the full me with no setbacks. Most times when you sign with a real estate office, seasoned agents are not interested in sharing too much of their knowledge. It's definitely very competitive! Plus, their time is limited. I love being known in my community as a kind and giving person.

Because I am! I'm the girl that lights the room up and makes people smile. I attribute my success to my mindset and pure heart.

In 2013, Craigslist was still a platform that people used to sell homes. Agents were using it and we could see the For Sale by Owner (FSBO) homes as well. As I was building my listing portfolio, all my listings were being added to the websites, just as today. I signed up with Zillow as a premier agent.

I was buying expired and FSBO leads and working my sphere and neighborhood. One day, as I was working in my little productivity booth, I noticed that one of my listings was advertised on Craigslist under another agent's name. The agent was a top producer in our office. I looked in disbelief at the ad that was asking people to call them with any questions about the house. At this moment in my career, I would handle the situation differently, but at that point in time I was very upset. If someone advertises your listing, they should include your name, or your company's name. Courtesy of Yoana Nin Realty was a must! They cannot promote themselves as listing agents for a home they did not list. How would you approach this today? I immediately went to the operating principal and made my point. She listened and told me that the office was allowing this type of practice with one condition: the listing agent had to be notified in advance! Since that was not the case, it was confirmed that the agent was wrong in his belief that he could do whatever he wanted with my listings. If he had called me ahead of posting my listing, I would have considered it. It could have been a win-win situation overall, with him bringing awareness and potential buyers. But he didn't! It was the first time in my life that I felt that type of anger.

When you cannot control your state of unhappiness and you stay negative, you don't help your situation. Without any personal communication between the two of us, the situation was resolved after a week or so. As my own boss, I started to carefully watch everything that was happening with my business.

What I understand now is that there is a difference between an agent who "wishes" to be in the business and an agent who "wants" to be in the business. I was not taken seriously.

As most agents close four to five transactions per year, the mega agents were looking at me as an unimportant piece that would probably disappear soon. But that year I closed nineteen homes with one delay, so pretty much twenty homes. My hard work was definitely paying off, so anyone attacking my life, income and hard work was threatening mama bear. I was having small wins every day, both personally and professionally. My confidence was skyrocketing. Here's a piece of advice; if you are in this business, and you are experiencing any sort of injustice, solve it gracefully. I would, at this moment. Also, instead of asking what could go wrong, always focus on what could go right. As a winner in the game of life, developing traits and mastering your mindset are key to your success. How do you stand out from the crowd? That authentic YOU will always resonate with your people, so do not give it away for anything!

The fact that I was so powerful and so blunt in that first year earned me a reputation in the office and with my clients. I always visualized one hundred thousand dollars as an income for that year. Having a good financial goal really helped me stay on track. Do you visualize your future and your finish line in life? How would you paint your next year?

It's needless to say that all of our friends and family were thrilled for our success. Winners check the box and never stop building that momentum. If I had stopped every time I had someone deny my services or if I had decided to move back to Romania, my whole life would have been different. It's the passion, the winning state of creating your own luck that will differentiate you from your competition. Don't negotiate your goals! Fight for them with every piece of your being and always learn more.

"We are what we think. All that we are arises with our thoughts. With our thoughts, we make the world."—Buddha

Be the expert in your craft. How much do you read? What have you learned about the real estate market recently? When setting your goals, make them specific. Here is an example: I want to make two hundred thousand dollars by December 3rd, 2021. My plan is to wake up at 5 a.m., run for twenty minutes, take a shower, meditate for ten minutes, drink coffee and eat breakfast with kids, then start work at 9 a.m. Every step of the day and week should be executed. Don't let anyone determine what is important to you.

In this business you get so many texts and emails, and if you do not focus on your daily priorities, your clients or friends' lives and their requirements will always win. Have a plan to execute. And when you lead gen, that's all you do. When you create videos, that's it. No other activity.

With your action and income, time should prevail. When you walk, leave your phone behind. Just relax! Don't try to multitask. Focus on one thing at a time and create an emotional relationship with your dreams and your goals. Think about Taylor Swift. That woman never ceased to reinvent herself. She never stopped working, even after she won a Grammy. Having a goal means turning the process of reaching it into a lifestyle for the duration of time it takes to achieve it. Don't stop when things don't go the way you assumed they would.

Chapter Eight

Phoenix

On January 7, 2014, I turned thirty-four years old. It was the day my grandma was buried and the day I got pregnant with my son. The burning desire to have a baby never died in our hearts. Do you think you would have decided to have a baby now that your career was taking off? Can you put yourself in my situation? We had barely any money in our savings, were working nonstop (but loving it), and finally feeling like we were up to something great. We were definitely planning for our future, growing a business and creating a retirement exit. I could have doubted the need for another child, but it was not in my nature.

I told my family I was pregnant in February, and my mom was a bit stressed about it. As a mother, I totally understand. She suffered greatly when we lost our second baby. In her heart, the worry of me going through a dramatic situation was definitely greater than the potential success of having another grandchild. It's funny how we let past traumas affect our present moments. Again, I totally understand her reaction! However, we were exuberant. I'm not sure what it is about me, but I can assure you that nothing dramatic lasts long within myself. I don't "carry" things for too long. Now I may have some small issues, drunken monkeys that I would still like to see gone, but besides those, I am free of heavy weights on my shoulders.

Around the same time, my company announced the KW family reunion that was happening in Phoenix, Arizona. It is the biggest event for agents-where founders of the company present the yearly real estate data, along with future predictions. Awards are given for nationwide achievements within the company. I had to go. Everyone was psyched about it, so my intention was set.

"I like getting myself into the situation that I desire and then I start planning."—Yoana Nin

My belly was growing, and my business was thriving. The reunion was a way to breathe some fresh air, to get to know other agents for potential referrals, and to have some fun with the agents in my office. Life was good.

Do you often see people celebrate anything before having success? Have you ever seen a happy poor person? How about a homeless dancing free? It's really hard to imagine having wealth, clients, and success without being there already, but that's my one key to success. Ever since I was planning or applying for a BFA theater and film, which was at the age of fifteen, I envisioned myself on stages under the bright lights. That image is still in my head, but now the stage has changed. There's a lot of confidence that I want to instill in you. I want you to be happy now, just as happy as I am, even though you don't have all those closings yet. Through daily visualization and mindset training, you will be able to make as much money as you want. But unless you are already happy with what you have NOW, even if it's little, the increased amounts of money will not make you feel accomplished. And it's not about what you WANT, as much as it's about what you ARE. If you envision something that is far from who you are, keep envisioning. If it's not real, it's... Fake!

Once you understand the power of gratitude in the now, once you envision already being there, the universe will open up to you. Never forget that we are energy, pure energy, and God is within all of us. We can heal our souls, we can change our lives, we can be as successful or stressed as we decide to be. It's your choice alone. There is no magic formula.

Anyone trying to sell you the top five secrets, or whatever they're trying to sell you, is really into getting your money.

"Believe nothing, no matter where you read it, or who said it, no matter if I have said it, unless it agrees with your own reason and your own common sense."— Buddha Siddhartha Guatama Shakyamuni

The clients and closings were rolling, and my energy level and aliveness were at the top. I still had some stress when I was getting back pain. Unintentionally, I was associating back pain with blood loss and miscarriage, but every day was a new day and just being alive was a privilege. I knew it was a boy, but I could not think of a name. None of us could. Looking up baby names was a hobby now. Every night we would look at names online and Anaïs would pick her top favorites. Morning sickness was not fun, but it did not disturb my overall work.

The day to travel for the reunion came fast. As I was saying goodbye to my family, I was thrilled to leave and breathe fresh air for a change. The shift from daily similar activities to a week filled with excitement was happening and nothing was going to stop me from having loads of fun!

I did not realize how much energy I would need to go through each day. We were starting at 9 a.m. or earlier and classes were happening all day long. I was able to choose which classes I took and an overwhelming feeling was slowly starting to happen. Mentally, I felt like I was a baby learning to read. I was meeting agents who were closing more than one hundred deals per year and making millions, especially if they were from California. So, my success seemed insignificant.

It's never too early or too late to start going to seminars or learning new ways to improve your business, but your mind has to be open to receiving it all. I thought I was ready, but it might have been a bit early considering it was my first year. However, the energy was exactly what I was longing for despite my entire body screaming for rest. It was like a mental Nirvana.

As the fourth day approached, I was starting to have some sort of discharge. No details needed, right?

If you're a woman, you know. As much as I tried to focus on all the data, my mind was shifting into fear mode. "I'm not ready to lose this baby. No way." Breathe, Yoana, breathe! That night, the North and South Carolina awards were being given. I got to my hotel at 7 p.m. and immediately jumped into the bathtub. There was no way I was going to participate. I could barely walk, let alone get dressed again and put a happy smile on my face. While lying in bed, I called Mihai and shared my little discharge news. I wasn't crying, but my level of anxiety was going through the roof. My face was red, my hair was messy, and my soul was agitated. Sharing my feelings with my husband helped me calm down a bit and his suggestion to not be alone in case something was about to happen was more than valid. So, I decided to throw something on and find out where this awards ceremony was being held. Looking exactly like I just got out of bed, I stepped out of my hotel room and called an agent friend for information on where the awards were being held. I slowly walked there, counting every step and feeling every bit of back pain. As I entered the room, I found myself ashamed of how I looked. Everyone was wearing nightgowns, sparkles, elegant shoes, purses, jewelry, etc.

I felt the urge to turn back and cry, but my need to be surrounded by people was greater than my urge to escape. As I dove deep into my chair, I heard the presenter on stage announce the first award. "Rookie of the year for 2013 goes to…" What was happening? My face was all over the room, on all the screens. Everyone started clapping, standing up, and cheering for me. I had no idea what to do and my colleagues gently helped me stand up and prompted me to go on stage and receive the Rookie of the Year award for the regions. I still get goosebumps when I look back at that moment.

My feet were trembling, my stomach was in pain, and my head was spinning.

I have never felt that amount of pride and confusion at the same time. As I stepped on stage and held my award, I forgot I actually had to leave the stage as well. I must've stayed there for a long period of time as someone came to walk me down and show me the way to where I was supposed to take pictures with someone important. To this day, I do not know who that lady was. I hope she's still important. After all of my colleagues congratulated me, I found myself walking back to my hotel alone. My family was not there to celebrate with me, and I was missing them like crazy. Fame lasts a couple of minutes, and then reality kicks in. What's next? How was I going to sleep? Was my back still hurting? Happily, not anymore. My shift in focus and the exuberance of winning such an important award took the pain and worry away. At 6 a.m., I woke up and started walking the streets in search of a good breakfast place. Since my husband was asleep during the awards, I could not speak to him and I was more than eager to tell him what had just happened. I quickly texted that I won the Rookie of the Year award and that I couldn't wait to talk to him.

As I sent that text, there was a surreal energy that filled my body and a voice that whispered in my ears, "This child will live. His name shall be Phoenix." It was my second encounter of this nature. An encounter with the SOURCE. By this point, I was crying alone on the street. It was not something I felt comfortable doing. Being vulnerable in public was not something my strong spirit was used to allowing. I somehow knew then that my mission was above myself.

Chapter Nine

Will you survive as an agent?

My mission is to dedicate my teachings to those who need guidance in real estate and to people that are willing to take the best they have inside them and turn it into a masterpiece. I want you to be filled with grace, with peace, with passion and with your own vision. No matter what your vision is, you can achieve it and begin your journey right now. Just get rid of limitations, self-induced fear, stress, and always be in a state of accepting things for what they are right now. Fighting what you don't know is not worth it, so why ponder over things you cannot change? Take control of your destiny. Build your systems. Be aware of your industry and the changes that are occurring and experience the intensity and pleasure of building your business.

I'm assuming you have some social media accounts. When was your online identity born? Mine was born eleven years ago, but as a realtor, I only started using Facebook properly about three years ago. When I say properly, I mean that I actually started creating ads, developing a plan for becoming a presence, and generating hundreds of leads that turned into clients. We learned how to create our own ads and spend as much money as we wanted on them. It took a lot of coaching, but we finally did it! Now, getting three closings a year from Instagram or Facebook does not mean that you actually have an online presence! It takes work. They say that building a brand takes around 8 years. As a realtor, I highly suggest that you focus on a platform that gives you joy and master it. Use it to your benefit. Post content that's natural and has humor and taste. If you identify with your people, if you can relate to their problems (and deeply care), they will notice you.

"BE CONSISTENT in everything you do, both in life and in your line of work. And be happy about being consistent."— Yoana Nin

It's amazing what we can do nowadays with a valuable online reputation! But online is not everything, right?

Proximity is also KEY! Meeting people face to face has never been more profound in my opinion. You can buy for sale by owner or expired leads and cold call to schedule appointments. You can go door knocking, which is free. You can do open houses, you can meet referrals, and you can pay for online leads. There's so much to choose from! Just be yourself. No matter what you decide to do, be yourself and people will be drawn to you.

REMEMBER: "likes" online, don't buy or sell with you! Ultimately, we all need to make money, to sell homes and have people buy homes. I had one year of COMPLEXITY and turmoil in 2018 as I was feeling overwhelmed by wanting to be on all the platforms to get business. But when the posts are not organic, there is NO return! The moment I agreed to just letting go, the moment I really provided value without expecting anything in return–the shift occurred. I am currently running three ads on Facebook and I upload posts on YouTube. I plan to start running ads there, shortly.

DANGER ALERT!

Have you ever looked at the amount of time you spend online? And if yes, what is the return? Do you notice how everyone wants to get into real estate, thinking they will make a lot of money and have time for themselves? The thing is that when you are your own boss, you need to be strategic and careful with how you spend your time.

"Never Exchange time for money!"—Nadęem

Being on Facebook for hours and looking at everyone's clothes does not get you too far in real estate, unless you are some marketing guru who comments on everyone's posts and then follows up with them for the rest of their lives. BUT THAT'S A FULL-TIME JOB! Instead, if you focus on two great conversations or connections, you might be better off.

Never exchange time with money, always exchange money for money! Since 2017, we have invested thirty thousand dollars into coaching with the best of the best; for knowledge. Instead of paying my company, I took the money and invested in our own brand. It was my choice! It was best for my business and personal freedom.

If you want to be known in your area, if you want to be relevant within your community and get people to recognize your face and call you, action is needed. You have to determine exactly when you will start posting regular weekly videos. If videos are not your thing, then what is? What makes you stand out? Blogs? Instagram? LinkedIn? Tik Tok? Are you diverse enough in the way you lead gen? You have to focus on your present, with your future in mind! Make your videos and posts fun and don't just show your listings.

Our kids are twelve and five. They go to school and are involved with their peers. They also enjoy sports, such as soccer and rock climbing. I happily connect with other moms and show that side of me on social media. My husband loves playing squash, which is something fun that people connect with. I am sure you have plenty of great things that make you stand out!

"The Only impossible journey
is the one you never begin"—
Anthony Robbins

The agents that embrace the change are the ones that will survive.

On my end, I feel very comfortable in front of the camera, and I love providing market updates.

Our listing presentations are based on the marketing that we provide online and the number of views our listings have, both on Facebook and on YouTube. My CRM database (Liondesk) receives email videos and video text messages weekly or every ten days. I also love sending jokes to my sphere, my people. I tailor everything based on my personality. I don't like cold calling, but I do it sometimes because most people that come into our database want to hear from me, and not from somebody else. As a new agent, I would not eliminate this method. However, with where the world is going, being online and working towards your brand can be more effective. Content on YouTube brings amazing clients who are ready to purchase with me as soon as possible. They already know my personality, so there's no need for convincing. That's what online presence and creating virtual trust means.

Let's see how open you are to something new, and forget about social media, as that is a very broad conversation. I challenge you to do a quick exercise. Talk to me about how open you are to embrace the new ways of doing business. Write yourself a letter that you will look at one year from today. Make sure you date it! Tell yourself everything, with brutal honesty. What do you think you need to do now in order to become successful? Remember that taking action will help you to shift your opinion in a big way.

The results of taking action will affect not just your life, but other people's lives too. Stay in "alive" mode.

Dear me,

Let me just start by saying that I love myself just the way I am.

I hope you had fun writing your letter, and I hope you are looking forward to reading it next year. As you can see, things change fast, and life is very unpredictable. You may need to change your ways and adapt in order to achieve success.

Allow me to share some money tips with you, coming from a wonderful human being, Esther Hicks. This is a post I found online, that encompasses all I want to share with you, so I am taking the freedom to quote here:

http://www.ilanelanzen.com/personaldevelopment/the-law-of-attraction-and-money-10-big-tips-from-esther-hicks/

MONEY TIPS FROM ESTHER HICKS:

Tip 1: The Better Your Story Gets, The Better Your Life Gets

The rich just get richer. We've all heard that before, and we all believe it because we've seen it. But why do they get richer? Could it be because the story they tell themselves is so good that they can't help but attract the circumstances, people, and situations into their life that make it even better? Or alternatively, think of someone who has no money and constantly tells a story about how they are broke and will never make enough money to pay the bills and live the life they want to live. Isn't it true that they attract negative experiences into their life that helps their story thrive today, tomorrow, and the next day after that? Even if they get some money in their life, their negative story ensures that they lose it in some way or another.

When you create a story of lack or desperation around yourself, you contradict your desire for wealth. And the Law of Attraction says that you can't have it both ways. You can't focus on what you don't want and then get what you do want. If your story is making you feel bad or desperate, then you can't allow wealth into your experience.

So, what can you do? Esther Hicks says that you need to tell the story you desire and then strengthen your story by visualizing what it is like to be living it. By doing this, you feel better about yourself and your life, and because you feel better, the details of your life will start to improve. You will start to see more positive circumstances, people, and situations in your life, and you will take chances that increase your wealth because you will believe in your story and the possibilities that lay ahead for you.

Tip 2: You Get What You Give Your Attention To

Esther Hicks says that for everything you want, there is a counterpart that you don't want. When you focus on what you don't want, even if it's in an effort to get it out of your life, it always comes closer to you. This is because whatever you give your attention to, you get. Therefore, you need to focus on what you want and NOT what you don't want.

Instead of focusing on your bills, focus on how you can bring more than enough money into your life to pay bills.

Instead of focusing on the low pay you receive at work, focus on increasing your pay, getting a raise, or building a business that earns you more and more every month.

Instead of focusing on your bank balance, focus on your desire to have a large bank balance that gives you the freedom to do whatever you want, whenever you want.

Always put your attention on what you want, because when you put your attention on what you don't want, the Law of Attraction says that you will attract more of what you don't want.

Tip 3: Life Is On Your Side

If the Law of Attraction were working perfectly for you, then you would be telling everyone you know, including yourself, that life is on your side. You would feel lucky. You would feel like no matter what you did, things were going to work out. You would have confidence that everything coming into your life, both good and bad experiences, was there to help you attract the type of life you want.

That's how you need to feel now. Even if you are in a place that could be better, you need to remember that life is on your side and the Law of Attraction is constantly working to attract what you want most in your life. So as long as you tell a good story and focus on what you want, life is on your side. Everything is working out for you. Everything is lining up so that you can get what you want.

For example, I know a few people who were fired and in a very bad spot financially in life. The ones that held on to the belief that they were let go from their job in order to move towards a better job that provided them with more of what they wanted, ended up in a much better place afterwards. The Law of Attraction ensured it. But the ones that got down on themselves and believed that the loss of their job reflected who they were, ended up in situations that continued to prove their story.

Life is always on your side. If you are using the Law of Attraction to attract what you do want, then it is coming, even if it hasn't arrived yet. Remember that and you will feel much better about where you are now and what is coming to you.

Tip 4: Appreciation Is Key To The Law of Attraction

Gratitude and appreciation are different vibrational states. This is something I've recently started to understand, and it's amazing at how your life changes once you get this simple truth.

Esther Hicks says that when you are focusing on gratitude, you often still have some focus on the struggle or what you don't want. For instance, if you are grateful that you just made enough money to pay your bills, you are always focused on the fact that you barely made enough money to pay your bills. That causes you to have a lower vibration where it's hard to attract what you do want in your life.

Appreciation, on the other hand, is the same vibration as love according to Esther. It's allowing you to acknowledge what is happening, what you are seeing, the people in your life and everything else, through the eyes of the Source. It puts you in the energetic flow where you are able to attract more of what you want easily because the lack of resistance.

Therefore, focus on appreciating everything in life. Recognize how amazing everything is in your life. Appreciate the people who are there for you. Appreciate the circumstances that arise and help you understand more about yourself and what direction you need to go in. Make appreciation an important part of your everyday life.

Tip 5: Do What Works For You

A lot of us live our lives based on what other people want. When it comes to wealth, we try to make other people happy as we make choices about our career, how we spend our money, how we save our money, and how we feel about money. But it's not your role to do what works for other people. It's your role to do what works for you. That's the only way the Law of Attraction can work to attract what you truly want most in your life.

If you are focused on what other people want or think, there is a hint of resistance holding back what YOU want most. You are debating with yourself if your desires are correct, and because your attention is shifting back and forth, you are not able to focus on what you truly want and align yourself with your desires.

I know that other people can be opinionated about money and wealth, but once you decide that you are doing your life for you, and not them, it becomes easier to ignore their opinions and live on your terms.

If you are in a relationship where you both have very different opinions about wealth, then you need to find a way to compromise that works for your desires. Conflict will keep you focused on what you don't want, and that's when the Law of Attraction will bring in more of what you don't want.

Tip 6: Make The Best Out Of A Bad Situation

Right now, things are happening in your life because of your vibrational state. Esther says that your vibration is offered because of your thoughts. Therefore, you need to find thoughts that feel good if you want to attract things into your life that feel good.

Esther offers the advice to look for the best-feeling aspects of any situations. If you must give your attention to something, find something to feel good about.

For instance, focus on the fact that you can put food on the table. Or focus on the fact that you have a roof over your head and money has helped you do that. This will help you have good thoughts that will help you attract more things to think and feel good about in your life.

She further suggests that you pivot yourself from bad to good feelings whenever possible. You can do this by looking for a better-feeling way to approach a situation.

Tip 7: Stop Thinking In Terms Of Shortage

When it comes to money, don't buy into myths that tell you there is not enough money to bring wealth into your life. If you do, then you will be creating negative thoughts and feelings towards money, and you will attract more shortage into your life.

And when it comes to the time, don't tell yourself that you don't have enough time left to create the wealth you want. If you do, you will definitely keep yourself stuck in a state of not being able to create the life you want.

There are many stories of people creating wealth out of nothing. There are many stories of people creating the life they want at all ages. Think in terms if "I can because life is on my side," not "I can't because there is not enough…" and you will find that life feels better and more things, people, and experiences, come into your life to help you get to where you want to be.

Tip 8: There Are Only Two Ways To Look At Money-lack or abundance

There is only lack or abundance. If you are focused on lack, then the Law of Attraction will bring you more lack of money. If you are focused on abundance, then the Law of Attraction will bring you more abundance.

Esther says that you might be assuming you are focused positively on money when you say things like "I want more money," but the truth is that you are feeling some sort of fear as you speak these words, and therefore you are really talking about not having enough money. And the Law of Attraction will bring you more of not enough money.

Tip 9: Financial Success Does Not Require Hard Work

When you buy into the belief that you need to work your butt off in order to acquire wealth, then the Law of Attraction says that you cannot get wealthy without working your butt off! Think about that for a second. The one belief could hold you back from attracting wealth unless you are willing to spend hours every day working hard.

Esther says that financial success is not about hard work, it's about being in the right alignment of thought. Therefore, adopt the belief that with the right mindset, thoughts, and feelings, you will do what needs to be done to attract wealth into your life. Then, you can start to keep your awareness open for what needs to be done next and let the Law of Attraction bring you the wealth you desire for being in alignment.

Tip 10: You Don't Need Money To Attract Money

Esther says that you don't need to have money to attract money. Wealth comes from being in alignment with Source. It comes from thinking positive thoughts about money and the rest of your life. It comes from feeling appreciation and having positive beliefs about yourself and what is possible in life.

Therefore, if you don't have any money in your life right now, you are not excluded from creating wealth in your life. The Law of Attraction is there to work for you, and when you start focusing on creating wealth, you will be given ways to create it, no matter where you are now.

Does all of this make sense to you? How do you feel after reading this? Since I hope it inspired you, I'd like to take you through another exercise. Promise you will look deep into your heart and you won't make anything up. Truth is the key! Please answer these questions without thinking twice.

What's your story?

Why are you in real estate?

How long do you see yourself doing real estate?

How healthy are you?

What's your value proposition?

Do you help your community?

Do you see yourself as an educated person?

Would you hire yourself?

Are you willing to go above your limiting beliefs and create a brand?

Would you like to leave a legacy behind?

Are you in this game for the long haul, in good and in bad?

How do you take rejection?

Do you love salespeople?

When was the last time you looked at your numbers?

How much time do you spend on yourself daily?

How much quality time do you spend with your loved ones?

If you could establish your brand right now, what would differentiate you from other realtors?

Do you invest in coaching?

Do you know where most of your clients are coming from?

Do you read often?

Have you ever helped a family member/friend buy or sell a house?

Are you still in a good relationship with that friend/family member?

Do you fancy having a big team?

Are you a broker?

Are you informed about all the loan programs that are out there?

What will you do in a SHIFT to stay in the business?

The Covid-19 pandemic is happening. Are you panicking?

Now that you have answered all of these questions, let me throw one more at you: have you ever attended an event organized by Tony Robbins? At his most recent Business Mastery in Palm Beach, Florida, there were two thousand attendees.

The attendees ranged from very small businesses to multi-millionaires who wanted to master their craft and increase revenue. Within a twelve to sixteen-hour day, Tony and his guests were able to take us through different emotional and mental exercises. My brain was on fire! We were dancing, jumping, screaming, and applauding. We learned about finances, branding, marketing, mindset, and all that makes a business survive challenging times. The room was cold, but I can assure you that every person in there was burning.

The passion that Tony has is overwhelming. He's the man that had it all, lost it all, got everything back, and branded himself to a point where he will live eternally through his soon to be completed hologram. In my opinion, Tony's burning desire is one hundred percent aligned with his vortex. To be as serving oriented as Tony Robbins is purely magical. He was there all five days, giving energy and wisdom. Do you think he needed to be present? Definitely! We were expecting him. And for his organization, the core principle is adding value. We were his clients. Each of us paid ten thousand dollars to be there. Do the math! He emphasized the importance of being surrounded by people that can lift you up. The core of the program was about leading your business effectively, efficiently and profitably to thrive in any economic time. We were inspired to determine our life, and enterprise visions.

Also, I was reminded that I am still a business operator instead of an owner.

Did you know that eighty-seven percent of businesses are gone if the founder disappears? Did you know that you always have to innovate? Finding a way to better meet your client's needs is progress, adding good marketing leads to success. Here are some other amazing takeaways: effective leaders spend less than five percent of their time on the problem and ninety-five percent of their time on the solution. Effective leaders know that resources are never the problem, it's always a question of resourcefulness. The core of a successful business is to create a vision beyond the moment, no matter how tough the moment is. Extraordinary people see something that no one else sees and take advantage of it.

Tony said that the only true competitive advantage in today's changing market and economy is NOT having a business plan but having a business MAP that can take you from where you are to where you want to be. If you want to be wealthy, start your map and master your mind. Remember: when you are in your heart, you're smart. When you are in your head, you're dead! Regardless of whether you are a starter agent or someone that has a huge team and mega production, a crisis can happen. These are the triggers that can lead to a crisis: change in competition, technology, economy, culture, customer's lives, employees' lives, and your life stage. So be prepared, be present in all circumstances and work on your marketing and innovation! As someone who went through recession and understands the value of being your own boss, I highly recommend working with passion and putting your all into it.

"I stay ready, so I don't have to get ready. I stay inspired so I don't have to get motivated"— Yoana Nin

Especially with COVID-19, real estate (as we knew it) became a struggle for those who are not into innovation and technology. But struggle can turn into productivity and profit with the right mindset.

Are you ready for this?

Chapter Ten

Being a Realtor during Covid-19. Agony vs ecstasy: your choice

Are you ready to be amazing and create magic? Today, while people are dying, kids are starving and races are fighting against each other, the Universe experiences renewal. I do not focus on the virus, recession, or fear! Not today, not tomorrow or any other time. I advise you to try to do the same. It does not mean that you should not take into consideration all that is happening. But what good will panic do to you? Besides the fact that you need to understand the real estate market, reacting with stress will not get you more closings. Inform your sphere, be the knowledgeable agent, keep up with the rates, keep up with changes in qualification criteria, and take it day by day with ease. Focus on the magic of finding your truth and following up with potential clients. Spend time with them on the phone, asking questions about their life, their situation, and their fears. Nothing will be more magical than quality time spent with the people that need your help right now.

As much as these are very strange times and races fight against each other, there is a reason for everything. Most people have lost their balance; they do not know why they do what they do, don't really feel like they have a purpose, and run away from their inner calling.

As for myself, as much as the world might see me as an "expert", I see beauty in having a beginner's mind.

I see the charming value that it brings to my conversations with every potential client. I see endless possibilities in a fresh mind and genuine care. If you need help as an agent, ask for support without ego, as there are many people out there that you can serve. It's so tiring and so draining to always "have" to generate clients. The main reason is the fact that there is no joy in most of the "client-generating" activities that agents nowadays do.

There is no juice in pushing people to use your services. It's not about hard work, it's about the way you approach things, the way you see yourself, your values and your strengths. If you find yourself in a bad mood one day, please stop crying over your shoulder. Get yourself out of that state and move on.

Do you want money? Let it flow your way. There are plenty of millionaires that are getting richer today. While you watch the news for three hours per day and cry over the future, they are making the money you could totally use for your family. Seek exciting activities and clients that make you want to meet them. Don't settle for less than what you are worth. Really, money is just money. But you need to take some action in order to gain confidence and in order to be a pro! Be creative, tickle your spirit and don't be afraid of being judged.

To fulfill my dream of coaching realtors, I'm currently creating a self-mastery course for real estate agents. You see, I have absolutely no clue what my course will look like. I have been home, like all of you, trying to do my very best with the kids and clients. I sometimes feel like I will go crazy, but it's mostly because of the lack of options I have when it comes to going places.

I'm grateful for our backyard, our pool, and our trampoline. I'm grateful that my mom was here for the last few months and helped with chores and watching the babes. I did not block my fears when they came upon me. Rather, I redirected them and consciously sent them away. My course is not ready, even though I had a time frame for when it should've been available. But I love myself and understand this situation. Stress will not make me move faster but kill me slowly. Stop worrying. I know it's not easy!

But using meditation to calm your mind daily does really help. Also, regardless of the situation, do not drop your fees. They are a filter for the type of people that you actually want to attract. You need to stay calm, healthy and take tiny steps towards your dream life.

Another thing that I'd like to touch on is that working long hours does not mean shit. It's a wrong concept that was implemented in your brain by this crazy system. If you are of no benefit to yourself and feel down, what is the point in staying in front of your laptop like a zombie? Go for a run or do stuff that makes you feel rejuvenated.

During this pandemic, I took some time to really look at how my kids have developed and how their personalities have grown. I noticed many things that I wouldn't have noticed if I was gone all the time. I listened to my mom and learned more about my grandparents. I enjoyed the sound of silence and I still earned a good amount of money.

If you think your family is the most important thing in your life, look at your calendar and tell me how much time you spend with them daily? Do you have any time blocked for your loved ones? Did you check your daily activities in the last fourteen days? How about you start tracking your hours spent at work vs with family starting tomorrow? I know one thing: you won't lie to yourself, unless you are in complete denial about who you are as an individual and as an agent. If you spend too much time on activities that bring you no return and your family barely sees you, change is needed asap!

"Lost, yesterday, somewhere between sunrise and sunset, two golden hours, each set with sixty diamond minutes. No reward is offered for they are gone forever."—Horace Mann

I am fearless with my goals, with my dreams, and with the type of service I provide. I have a deep sense of confidence in my actions, in my ability to be my own boss, and in delivering mastery for my clients. I also know that I will do the same for the agents that I will coach. Since I thrive with being coached myself, I have a deep respect for the people that understand the need to become masters/pros in their profession. One simply cannot succeed alone.

There are many fears around money, sales in general, among realtors. But as I stated before, and as I hope you answered one of the questions in the book, if you hate sales, please understand that real estate is about having clients and closing deals. I know many real estate agents who make a lot of money and are very supportive and dedicated to helping others. If you simply cannot afford anything towards coaching, ask agents in your office to help and read a lot of books.

But most importantly, start telling people about yourself and get yourself in a position where you can make money. Show your clients how amazing you are. Offer them value that they have not seen before. Help them see real estate agents differently, as I am sick and tired of people thinking that our profession is easy and that we are all shallow. We, as real estate agents, are a very important part of people's lives. We highly contribute to the well-being of our economy. But please, do not fall for the people-pleasing bullshit that is going around. Sales do not mean manipulation. One does not need to have a high IQ in order to feel that you are selling yourself and you do not give a flying squirrel about their house, their life or their dreams. If you are genuinely interested in helping and making a difference, you'll get the deal.

I have never used scripts, or printed one listing appointment. I do everything on my laptop or Ipad. I research the neighborhood and past sales thoroughly. I ask a lot of questions and determine their motivation for selling. I assess what is needed so that I am able to provide advice on anything that needs addressing. I never withhold any information in fear of people using it and not getting the sale. My goal is not to become "friends" with my clients. My only goal is for my clients to never forget their experience. To achieve this, I need to be different and knowledgeable. Among all the agents in the world, there aren't too many that actually make a living in this profession. It takes patience, dedication, talent, vision, and a strong character. If you're a pussy that gets upset every time you hear a NO, leave this job.

You'll get your bottom kicked many times, and I expect you to get up and smile.

Walk through Hell with JOY and you will find success.

Your clients will pay you as much as you charge them in order to achieve their dreams. Their family's needs are your needs for the time that you are under agency agreement, so you better be involved and put your magic and knowledge at work. Partner with people that can help if they need help. Give them resources and leave them in awe. And if you feel that you failed at some point, do not worry. We all do. Perfection does not exist. Fail more, experience more, tweak more, ask more, live more! Enjoy the challenges that come with failing and succeeding. The goal is to enjoy every step of the way, not only the happy moments and closings.

As we are not employees, we are one hundred percent in control of every day, minute and hour. We wake up, get ourselves together and start the journey. Every day is a new day, and if you have an idea of where you want to be in this career, that's an amazing start. If you know what your lifestyle should be like in the next ten years, that's even better. Go work for it! Create it! Be great, create lasting memories and give your clients experiences, rather than just another sale or purchase. Also, ask for reviews. It's important to hear their genuine opinion, and it's important for the world to see your value. Sometimes I feel that most real estate agents are afraid of being criticized, and they are mortified by the idea that they might get a mediocre review on Zillow or Facebook. So what?

Do you think that a bad review will define you? Feel free to answer to their review and move on. Hopefully you will create the experience that will blow your client's mind away, but sometimes, especially when you do not listen to your instinct, you might end up with a client that is not the ideal one. And guess what, no commission check is worth your peace of mind and the struggles of closing the deal. What is important to remember is that you need to ask many questions when deciding on working with your clients. You are in charge, not backwards. Do NOT jump into showing them homes or dropping your commission. Never! Do not try to convince anyone of how amazing you are! Covid or not, crisis or not, follow your dream and keep your values!

Most people do not care anyway about what you have to offer. All they want to know is if you can help them. That's what happens when you are bombarded with questions about homes, values, details, etc.

"Don't ask what the world needs. Ask what makes you come alive and go do that. Because what the world needs is people who have come alive."—Howard Thurman

And nowadays, with all they can find online, you need to really be able to give them more than what they already found by Googling and Facebooking and Tweeting and so on. They think they know it all. They think they can buy and sell without you, and convenience firms are there to release the "struggle" and act faster than you can imagine.

So, what are you doing in the meantime? How will you prevail? Astonish them with your confidence and your energy. I will say it again and again: if you are dead inside and hope to make a living in this business or in any business-it's not going to work.

You might have some sporadic successes here and there. You might have some good years, but eventually you will find yourself tired, drained and lifeless. And nobody will want to hire you then. Life is too short to be wasted on activities that do not make us feel alive.

Lastly, here is a letter that I wrote to remind me how special I am.

To myself, the one that cannot sit still, the one that sometimes feels that all the world's problems are resting on her shoulders...

I know what you like the most. You like to swim in a lukewarm pool or lake or ocean. You enjoy listening to nature and quieting your mind. You love hikes and anything adrenaline related(besides looking down to the nothingness on a steep mountain hike). You would love to be a pilot(still, after all these years). You miss the stage on your pre-menstrual days, and some of your "old days" friends.

You feel that if something happened to your family you would die of pain. Every time one of them gets sick, you can't sleep and you make a whole drama out of it(even the slightest fever). You are restless in feeding them green drinks with chlorella, ashwagandha, turmeric and noni powder(and many more!)

Your soul never stops being alive, happy and compassionate. Your ego can be the biggest and then it can completely disappear, depending on the weather(for real). You love Zen and Buddhism; you like listening to people and believing in them.

You are a true friend to anyone that won your heart. You make people smile. If anyone attacks your beliefs of what is "right" in your opinion, you can get pretty agitated. But then you realize that nobody can make you feel sad or upset, unless you allow them to.

Yoana, you are a woman of integrity. You do have "something" against laziness and you feel that people should do things your way sometimes, which is not fine.

You are too energetic and spontaneous for your own good sometimes. You still need to learn to listen more, but your mouth simply likes talking and repeating "stuff".

But how I love you! You are alive. Truly alive. There is not one inch of your body that lives this life in a reactive mode. You tell things the way they are and you feel when others don't do things from the heart. Love is your mantra and joy is your key. I have to admit, I would choose you over many women out there...if I was a man.

Even though you are not the hottest woman out there, and your nose is a bit big, your way of hugging and singing and being crazy is amazing. And you're a great kisser. And you smell good(most days).

Oh, I almost forgot: you are not like every other woman. You don't care much about clothing and such. But you love massages. You want to be massaged all the time. Your husband knows best!

You also love perfumes. But generally, going shopping is never a priority. You would go out in nature and do fun stuff over any dress or purse or shoe. However, you do like shopping for the house, as you love staging and decorating. That never gets boring for you.

You're super intelligent, and creative. You don't give a flying squirrel about being politically correct. You live in the moment, so everything you say and do is because you want to get better, you want to learn more. That's the spirit!

To some extent, some people might think that you are always high or something, when really, you never used drugs.

The only drink you really enjoy is Jagermeister. That's your thing. The rest are not significant.

At 40, you achieved so much! You achieved greatness, as you kept the child within you. You're strong, passionate, dedicated and yourself. I love you Yoana. Keep rocking!

On the next page, you will see a letter that I wrote to myself in Romanian, whilst I was at Tony Robbin's Business Mastery. I was rushing as I wrote it. I didn't understand why it was so important at the time. They mailed it to us and I only just received it, six months later. I will not translate it for you, but reading it brings tears to my eyes.

Be the best versions of yourselves! Thank you for joining me through my joyful journey! Yoana

Jan 26, 2020

Dear lovely Amazing Yoana, Ioana,
și tot ceea ce ești tu,

Nu cred că atunci când te-ai uitat la ghioul ai
avut momente de confuzie în legătură cu ce ai în
inimă. Să nu uiți niciodată că acea fetiță este încă în
inima ta.

Ești o femeie extraordinară și ai dat atât de mult din
tine. E timpul să îți amintești că ceea ce simți este
adevărat. Tot binele din lume pe care îl vei împlini are
nevoie doar de relaxare și sisteme. Chiar dacă nu îți plac
mult e obligația ta să le înveți și să îi înveți și pe alții.

Tot ceea ce faci este obligația ta morală, le dau
cadoul experienței mele de aproape 40 ani. Sunt mamă,
femeie de afaceri, dar dincolo de toate aceste lucruri sunt
o fetiță simplă! O fetiță care va face tot ce va putea
să ajute alți oameni care trec prin momente grele.

Ioana, Yoana, iubita mea: ai o familie extraordinară,
oameni care te iubesc! Nu ai nevoie de nimic altceva!

10 lucruri pe care trebuie să te concentrezi:
   – Pune-ți țelele pe perete
   – program determinat
   – curs și carte   – fă sport regulat!
   – citește mai mult
   – numere
      – timp cu Miha și copiii individual
   – zâmbește, dansează
   – Te iubesc și mulți te iubesc și te vor iubi
   – Ai încredere în tine

REFERENCES

A quote by Buddha. (n.d.). Retrieved from https://www.goodreads.com/quotes/1270-there-is-nothing-more-dreadful-than-the-habit-of-doubt

Brown, R. M. (n.d.). Rita Mae Brown Quotes. Retrieved from https://www.brainyquote.com/quotes/rita_mae_brown_131927

Buddha. (n.d.). A quote from Sayings Of Buddha. Retrieved from https://www.goodreads.com/quotes/498520-no-one-saves-us-but-ourselves-no-one-can-and

Buddha. (n.d.). A quote by Gautama Buddha. Retrieved from https://www.goodreads.com/quotes/1349139-we-are-what-we-think-all-that-we-are-arises

Buddha, G. (n.d.). A quote by Gautama Buddha. Retrieved from https://www.goodreads.com/quotes/13132-believe-nothing-no-matter-where-you-read-it-or-who

Bushnell , N. (n.d.). A quote by Nolan Bushnell. Retrieved from https://www.goodreads.com/quotes/1503420-the-critical-ingredient-is-getting-off-your-butt-and-doing

Hemingway, E. (n.d.). A quote by Ernest Hemingway. Retrieved from https://www.goodreads.com/quotes/353013-i-like-to-listen-i-have-learned-a-great-deal

Hicks, E., & Hicks, J. (2006). The law of attraction: The Basics of the Teachings of Abraham. United States of America: Hay House.

Huntzinger, A. (2007). Guidelines for the Diagnosis and Treatment of Tick-Borne Rickettsial Diseases. American Family Physician, 76(1), 137.

Isherwood, C. (1966). Exhumations: Stories, Articles, Verses. London: Methuen.

Keller, G., Jenks, D., & Papasan, J. (2004). The millionaire real estate agent: its not about the money. New York: McGraw-Hill.

Kyokai, B. D. (n.d.). A quote from The Teaching of Buddha. Retrieved from https://www.goodreads.com/quotes/1267-the-secret-of-health-for-both-mind-and-body-is

Lama, D. (n.d.). A quote by Dalai Lama XIV. Retrieved from https://www.goodreads.com/quotes/74781-our-prime-purpose-in-this-life-is-to-help-others

Lauritsen, A. (2016). 100 Days Drive: The Great North American Road Trip. United States: CreateSpace Independent Publishing Platform.

Lazyyogi. (2012, September 25). The Lazy Yogi. Retrieved from https://thelazyyogi.com/post/32247835691/consider-the-trees-which-allow-the-birds-to-perch

Mills, C. (n.d.). "You never know how strong you are until being strong is the only choice you have." – Ca...: Inspirational quotes motivation, Inspirational quotes, Typography quotes. Retrieved from https://www.pinterest.co.uk/pin/448530444114483840/

Nadeem. (2019, May 3). 3 Benefits of Online Business To Earn Money On The Internet. Retrieved from https://gotryus.com/benefits-of-online-business/

Nin, A. (1992). Incest: From "A Journal of Love": The Unexpurgated Diary of Anaïs Nin. Houghton Mifflin Harcourt.

O'Brien, B. (2018, September 9). Dukkha: What Buddhists Really Mean by 'Life Is Suffering'. Retrieved from https://www.learnreligions.com/life-is-suffering-what-does-that-mean-450094

Radmacher, M. A. (2008). Live boldly: cultivate the qualities that can change your life. San Francisco, CA: Conari Press, an imprint of Red Wheel/Weiser, LLC.

Robbins, A. (n.d.). A quote by Anthony Robbins. Retrieved from https://www.goodreads.com/quotes/877199-the-only-impossible-journey-is-the-one-you-never-begin

Sudo, P. T. (2005). Zen 24/7: All Zen, All the time. San Francisco, CA: HarperOne.

Summers, K. (n.d.). 51 Parents Quotes to share and make you smile. Retrieved from https://www.wow4u.com/parents-quotes/

Suzuki, S. (n.d.). A quote by Shunryu Suzuki. Retrieved from https://www.goodreads.com/quotes/147808-the-most-important-point-is-to-accept-yourself-and-stand

Suzuki Shunryū. (2011). Zen mind, beginners mind: informal talks on Zen meditation and practice. Boston, MA: Shambhala.

The Law Of Attraction And Money: 10 Big Tips From Esther Hicks. (2016, December 8). Retrieved from http://www.ilanelanzen.com/personaldevelopment/the-law-of-attraction-and-money-10-big-tips-from-esther-hicks/

Vasilescu, I. (2015, March 4). Retrieved from https://www.dontpayfull.com/blog/a-wise-person-should-have-money-in-their-head-but-not-in-their-heart

Winfrey, O. (n.d.). A quote by Oprah Winfrey. Retrieved from https://www.goodreads.com/quotes/625783-create-the-highest-grandest-vision-possible-for-your-life-because